The
Gluten-Free
Asian Kitchen

The Gluten-Free Asian Kitchen

Recipes for Noodles, Dumplings, Sauces, and More

LAURA B. RUSSELL

Photography by LEO GONG

CELESTIAL ARTS
Berkeley

For Patrick
From those first garlicky snails at the
Red Rooster to breakfast sushi in Tokyo,
our two decades of dining adventures have
been second to none.
Cheers!

Contents

Introduction

A few years ago, I sat with my husband and two children in a local Chinese restaurant trying desperately to find something on the menu I could eat that was gluten free. Two women sat down at the table next to us and one of them proceeded to tell her dining companion that she was under strict doctor's orders to avoid gluten. A kindred spirit, I thought, until she laughed it off and stated authoritatively, "It's no big deal; I just can't order the noodles." My husband reacted calmly as I tried to jump out of my seat—and into their conversation—putting his hand on my arm to keep me in place while quietly shaking his head "no." "It's not your concern," he said.

Oh yes, it is.

My own experience with gluten intolerance started shortly after the birth of my second child. I started fighting off a bevy of bizarre neurological symptoms, beginning with localized nerve pain and eventually growing into facial numbness and paralysis of the left side of my face. At its worst, the numbness traveled down the entire left side of my body. Some of these symptoms remained firmly in place for a couple of years, while others retreated as quickly as they appeared; all were puzzling and scary. About four years into this, and not a single step closer to finding an answer, I turned my focus from fruitlessly searching for a diagnosis to improving my general health. I started a one-month elimination diet, cutting out most foods that were allergenic or inflammatory, including gluten, dairy, soy, corn, caffeine, alcohol, and sugar. Three weeks later, I felt better than I had in years and was completely symptom free. At the end of the month, I took that first bite of a much-missed bagel and—*whoosh!*—nearly instant facial numbness.

I had discovered my body's aversion to gluten.

At that point I stopped eating gluten completely, which includes anything containing wheat, barley, rye, or cross-contaminated oats. I don't have a problem with this when I'm eating at home, but the story changes once I walk out the front door. Dining in any restaurant can be difficult, but going out for Asian food remains my biggest frustration. As I soon discovered, many of the essential ingredients in Asian cooking are wheat-based. Dumplings, pancakes, and many types of noodles are blatant offenders, but it's the omnipresent sauces, quietly painting each bite with gluten, that are harder to avoid. Soy sauce, a condiment made from fermented soybeans and wheat, is an exceedingly common ingredient in Asian cooking. Other sauces, such as teriyaki sauce and some peanut sauces, are based on soy sauce. Hoisin sauce and oyster sauce are routinely thickened with wheat flour; hoisin sauce may also be sweetened with a wheat paste. In trying to dodge these roadblocks, it can be hard finding even a simple stir-fry that's safe to eat. Certainly over the past few years the whole concept of gluten-free dining has progressed at a rapid speed, but with much of the commercial focus on getting that bread, that pizza, or that cake back on the plate. But what about other foods that we all love, such as Japanese, Korean, and Chinese, which are some of my personal favorites? I decided that it's time to shine the spotlight on Asian cooking.

During my gluten-eating days, I frequented Asian restaurants in New York City, Portland, and San Francisco with great vigor. (Not to mention a revelatory food-focused visit to Tokyo with my husband.) As a recipe developer I gobbled up not only the delicacies set before me, but information as well. I studied menus, quizzed helpful chefs, and scoured markets in Chinatown, picking up a bit more knowledge each step of the way. Eventually I started cooking my way through Asian cookbooks at home, a fun and satisfying experience. By the time I had to give up gluten, I realized my newfound skills were critical to my continued enjoyment of Asian food. Any initial sadness I felt over losing gluten was trumped by my delight in knowing how to cook. I somehow felt like sharing this knowledge with other people in the same situation would make the whole ordeal worthwhile.

Gluten free or not, I want everything I eat to be delicious. And while dining out remains one of my favorite pastimes, if I can't find what I'm craving in a restaurant—more and more common since I went gluten free—then I cook it at home.

The one hundred recipes in this book originate from the Thai, Korean, Chinese, Japanese, and Vietnamese cuisines I love so much. My goal is not to reinvent the wheel or hand you a bunch of strange Asian-fusion concoctions, but to provide solid recipes for some of the great Asian foods you may find yourself missing since you've gone gluten free. In this book, I've tried to make old favorites accessible again, and I hope to introduce a few new ideas into the mix as well.

In creating this gluten-free Asian lineup, I found the recipes fell into three categories:

1. **Major overhaul:** Recipes that needed some type of big conversion to make them gluten free. This includes rethinking panko breadcrumb coatings, wheat-based thickeners, dumpling dough, batters, and traditional sauces.
2. **Tweaking/minor substitution:** Recipes that required a simple substitution to create a gluten-free version, such as using wheat-free tamari or gluten-free oyster sauce.

3. **Naturally gluten free:** Some recipes are gluten free by nature, specifically many fish sauce–based Thai and Vietnamese recipes. Generally, when I give you a naturally gluten-free recipe, I am hoping to introduce an ingredient or a technique that might be new to you. For instance, Korean rice cakes are gluten free, but maybe you're not familiar with them. Vietnamese salad rolls don't contain gluten, but you may appreciate instruction on using the rice paper needed to make them. Or, if you've already mastered salad rolls, perhaps you'll enjoy some of the other interesting ways you can use rice paper—as a crisp wrap for sautéed salmon, for example.

The resulting recipes are approachable and range from simple weeknight stir-fries to more time-consuming dumplings, perfect for the weekend. When you become more familiar with the gluten-free ingredients, you will eventually feel confident enough in your knowledge to take it outside the book, making appropriate gluten-free substitutions in any recipe you come across.

Because this is a gluten-free cookbook (and due to the nature of the topic, it's dairy free as well), I didn't want you to have concerns about lack of flavor, odd textures, or any feeling of missing out that people with food sensitivities are already so familiar with. So as part of the process of writing this book, I gathered about twenty friends, all avid gluten eaters, and asked them to taste the recipes as I developed them. The group offered great feedback and even tested the completed recipes in their own kitchens. The home testing garnered overwhelmingly positive results from adults and children alike. And except for the cooks, none was the wiser to the dishes' gluten-free status.

Thankfully, some large national chain restaurants are starting to offer gluten-free options on their Asian menus. But until more of the smaller, local Asian restaurants familiarize themselves with the fundamentals of gluten-free cooking and they are willing to source and pay for alternate ingredients, we're largely on our own. (And let's face it, the thought of strolling into a traditional Chinatown restaurant and asking for a gluten-free menu is fairly unrealistic: Can you please change your centuries-old recipes for me?)

Cooking a delicious Asian meal at home is well within your reach, and I will show you how. I'm handing you the spatula—now it's your turn to fire up the wok.

ONE Getting Started

When you go to the grocery store, do you even need a list? Or like most people, do you grab the same set of basics week after week? For many home cooks pressed for time, shopping has become a routine. The idea of shopping for unfamiliar ingredients, particularly those of a foreign cuisine, simply knocks many people out of their comfort zone. Add gluten-free restrictions to the mix and the prospect becomes downright daunting. What's a home cook to do? Relax, take a deep breath, and work with me.

When the task at hand seems intimidating, I find it best to break things down. In this chapter I've included a chart that will help you determine which Asian ingredients contain gluten and why and a guide to ingredients that not only defines what you need, but also points you in the best direction for locating it. While a few of the items require a trip to an Asian market, I tried very hard to use ingredients from well-stocked grocery stores and natural foods markets or co-ops. If you do have an Asian market in your town, though, take a field trip and explore what the market offers; it can be quite transporting. Asian markets offer a wealth of ingredients, often including an amazing produce section and a well-stocked seafood counter. Because the markets house so many unfamiliar ingredients, it may take a scouting trip or two to gain familiarity. Stroll through the aisles, read labels, learn something new.

For gluten-free brands of traditional gluten-laden sauces (soy sauce, oyster, hoisin), I feel more comfortable buying these from a regular grocery store or natural food market because the labels are in English. Label translation can end up with inaccuracies, a chance I'm not willing to take when my health is at stake. If your grocery store doesn't carry gluten-free brands of the most basic Asian sauces, request the products you need.

I grocery shop for sport, a practice my friends suggest is the exception to the rule. If you don't share my enthusiasm for shopping, keep your pantry stocked with some of the basics. Check out The Short List in this chapter for the most frequently used items in the book. Purchasing them all at once would be pricey, but consider building your collection to include these staples. Once in place, you can tackle a great many of the recipes after one quick stop for produce, tofu, meat, or fish.

Once you've navigated your way through the ingredients, you'll need to assess your equipment. Some people shy away from Asian cooking, thinking they need to purchase all kinds of specialty gear. Don't be surprised if I encourage you to buy a wok, but it's because it's fun to use, not because owning one is absolutely necessary. In the Tools and Techniques section I list the pots, pans, and tools I relied on when developing the recipes. You'll be pleasantly surprised to find most of them already in your kitchen— now go in there and get them dirty!

Identifying Sources of Gluten in Common Asian Ingredients

Avoiding gluten in Asian cooking is achieved only with great care and attention to detail. Some of the most common ingredients you will find in Asian recipes or restaurant dishes are listed below, followed by the reason each one may be off limits. Because gluten is found in all forms of wheat, barley, rye, and cross-contaminated oats, those are the ingredients to avoid. The biggest culprit is wheat, although barley and barley malt do make their way into some of these ingredients. I did not notice any rye, but you should still keep an eye out for it. Once armed with this information, you can feel comfortable making substitutions for the prohibited offenders in any recipe you come across. Solutions range from swapping the item for a homemade version, locating a gluten-free brand, or trying a similar alternative.

The gluten-free market is constantly growing and changing. Check your local grocery store for the products you need and request the ones that are missing. Your voice will get these products on the shelves. Very few of the items listed lack a gluten-free alternative, and hopefully in time it will be easy to locate everything we need. In the meantime, new brands appear frequently, but existing brands can change their ingredients. Remain diligent when it comes to label reading and contact companies directly if their labels need clarification.

As you know, gluten can appear in the most unexpected places. Many of the items below should be gluten free (cornstarch, fish sauce, rice vinegar) and nine times out of ten they will be. But it only takes that one surprise ingredient to throw you off course. Read every label, every time.

IDENTIFYING GLUTEN

INGREDIENT	GLUTEN STATUS	ALTERNATIVE	GLUTEN-FREE BRANDS*
Bean sauce, Chinese chile (soy or black)	Based on a fermented bean-and-wheat paste	Some brands are gluten free	Lan Chi (+), Lian How, Wei Chuan
Bean sauce, Thai yellow	Based on a fermented soybean-and-wheat paste	Yellow miso paste	Not available
Chili-garlic sauce/Sriracha	Some are thickened with wheat flour	Many brands are gluten free	Huy fong (+), Lan Chi (+), Sun Luck (+)
Chili sauce, sweet	Some are thickened with wheat flour	Many brands are gluten free	**A Taste of Thai, Grama's sweet chili sauce, Thai Kitchen**

*Brands listed in bold have a gluten-free label. The other brands do not include any ingredients that contain gluten on their labels. A plus symbol (+) indicates the company has confirmed that only gluten-free ingredients were used, even though not officially stated on the label. Brands change frequently; check your area for additional options.

IDENTIFYING GLUTEN

INGREDIENT	GLUTEN STATUS	ALTERNATIVE	GLUTEN-FREE BRANDS*
Cornstarch	Should be gluten free; check for additives	Substitute tapioca or potato starch in some cases	Readily available
Crab, Imitation (crab sticks, surimi)	Highly processed; often contains wheat as a binder	Real crab meat or a gluten-free brand with tapioca or rice starch binder	Fresh crab readily available at the fish counter
Curry paste, Thai	Should be gluten free; check for additives	Fresh Green Curry Paste (page 33) or a gluten-free brand	**A Taste of Thai, Thai Kitchen,** Mae Ploy
Curry roux	Blend of wheat flour, oil, and spices; present in packaged Japanese curry sauces and curry rice mix	Use curry powder; thicken with cornstarch and simmering (see Japanese-style chicken curry, page 156)	Not available
Dashi, instant	Powdered versions nearly always contain MSG, a questionable ingredient for many sensitive to gluten	Dashi (page 36)	Proceed with caution
Dumpling wrappers	Commercial pot sticker, wonton, egg roll, and gyoza wrappers are wheat-based	Pot Sticker dough (page 58) or rice paper wrappers	Wrappers not available; there are regional brands of gluten-free frozen dumplings
Fish sauce	Should be gluten free; check for additives	No alternative needed	Readily available
Ginger, pickled	Many contain preservatives, artificial coloring and flavorings—questionable ingredients for those highly sensitive to gluten	Pickled Ginger (page 35) or try a natural brand of pickled ginger	**The Ginger People**
Gochujang (Korean hot red pepper paste)	Contains wheat, barley, or both; even versions thickened with sweet rice flour instead of wheat still include barley malt as a sweetener	Not available	Not available
Hoisin Sauce	Usually thickened with wheat flour or sweetened with wheat paste	Some brands are gluten free	Dynasty (+), **Premier Japan, Wok Mei**
Kecap manis (thick, sweet soy sauce)	Based on soy sauce, which usually contains wheat	Use Kecap Manis Substitute, page 67	Use caution; import stickers often obscure ingredient lists
Kimchi	Sometimes thickened with a wheat-flour based slurry	Cabbage Kimchi (page 116) or a gluten-free brand	Available

*Brands listed in bold have a gluten-free label. The other brands do not include any ingredients that contain gluten on their labels. A plus symbol (+) indicates the company has confirmed that only gluten-free ingredients were used, even though not officially stated on the label. Brands change frequently; check your area for additional options.

INGREDIENT	GLUTEN STATUS	ALTERNATIVE	GLUTEN-FREE BRANDS*
Maggi seasoning	Many labels list wheat gluten, wheat, and wheat bran	Could substitute gluten-free tamari with a touch of gluten-free Worcestershire sauce	Not available
Mirin	Should be gluten free; check for additives	No alternative needed; can use mirin substitute (page 14)	Readily available
Miso	Barley-based miso (mugi miso) contains gluten; rice-based miso does not	Use rice-based miso paste, which is the most readily available type	Readily available
Noodles	Wheat noodles, egg noodles, ramen, somen, udon, and most soba contain wheat flour	Try rice noodles, cellophane (mung bean) noodles, sweet potato vermicelli, or 100% buckwheat soba	**Annie Chun's, A Taste of Thai,** Dynasty (+), **Thai Kitchen**
Noodles, rice	Dried rice noodles should be gluten free. Fresh rice noodles can contain wheat starch	No alternative needed	**Annie Chun's, A Taste of Thai,** Dynasty (+), **Thai Kitchen**
Noodles, soba	Buckwheat flour does not contain gluten, but most soba noodles are also made with a bit of wheat flour	Use 100% buckwheat soba	Eden (+), Mitoku (+)
Oyster sauce	Usually thickened with wheat flour, often contains MSG	Some brands are gluten free	Dragonfly, Lee Kum Kee's Panda (Green label only), **Wok Mei**
Panko (Japanese-style bread crumbs)	Made from bread; contains wheat	Try a sesame seed (Sesame-Crusted Salmon, page 137) or cornflake (Pork Tonkatsu, page 172) crust or a gluten-free brand	**Kinnikinnick**
Peanut sauce	Based on soy sauce, which usually contains wheat	Peanut Satay Sauce (page 31), or a gluten-free brand	**A Taste of Thai, San-J, Thai Kitchen**
Plum sauce	Can contain wheat flour or fermented wheat paste	Some are thickened with cornstarch or naturally with plum puree	Dynasty (+), Sun Luck (+), **Wok Mei**
Rice	Rice is inherently gluten free. Beware of seasoning packets	No alternative needed	Readily available
Rice, sticky	Also called sweet rice or glutinous rice because of its sticky nature; it is gluten free	No alternative needed	Available

*Brands listed in bold have a gluten-free label. The other brands do not include any ingredients that contain gluten on their labels. A plus symbol (+) indicates the company has confirmed that only gluten-free ingredients were used, even though not officially stated on the label. Brands change frequently; check your area for additional options.

IDENTIFYING GLUTEN

INGREDIENT	GLUTEN STATUS	ALTERNATIVE	GLUTEN-FREE BRANDS*
Rice paper wrappers	Made from rice flour and sometimes tapioca starch; should be gluten free	No alternative needed	Available
Rice vinegar (rice wine vinegar)	Should be gluten free; check for additives	No alternative needed	Readily available Marukan
Rice wine, Chinese Shaoxing	Often brewed with a combination of rice and wheat	Substitute dry sherry or a gluten-free brand	Available
Sake	Naturally gluten-free alcoholic beverage brewed from rice	No alternative needed	Readily available
Sambal oelek	Should be gluten free; check for additives	Sriracha or chili garlic sauce	Huy Fong (+)
Sesame oil	Should be gluten free	No alternative needed	Readily available
Soy sauce	Traditionally brewed from a combination of soybeans and wheat	Gluten-free soy sauce or gluten-free or wheat-free tamari	Hy-vee (+), Kari Out, (also see Tamari)
Tamari	A darker, richer soy sauce from fermented soybeans; may or may not contain wheat	Gluten-free soy sauce or gluten-free or wheat-free tamari	Many companies have both wheat and wheat-free versions; read the label carefully. **Eden, Koyo, Mitoku, Oshawa, San-J, Tree of Life**
Tea	Most unflavored tea is gluten free, however roasted barley tea is popular in many Asian cuisines	Green tea, black tea, oolong tea	Readily available; beware of barley tea in restaurants
Tempura batter	Usually based on wheat flour	Try a combination of rice flour and cornstarch or tapioca	Not available
Teriyaki sauce	Based on soy sauce, which usually contains wheat	Teriyaki Sauce (page 26) or a gluten-free brand	**Premier Japan, San-J**
Tofu	Plain, unseasoned tofu is gluten free	No alternative needed	Readily available
Wasabi	Grated fresh wasabi is gluten free, but hard to find. Check labels on tube and powdered versions; ingredients vary wildly	Some brands are gluten free	Available
Wheat gluten (Fu, mian jin, seitan)	Pure gluten, or gluten mixed with grains; used as a meat substitute	Not available	Not available

*Brands listed in bold have a gluten-free label. The other brands do not include any ingredients that contain gluten on their labels. A plus symbol (+) indicates the company has confirmed that only gluten-free ingredients were used, even though not officially stated on the label. Brands change frequently; check your area for additional options.

Stocking the Gluten-Free Asian Kitchen: A Guide to Ingredients

Shopping for ingredients has never been easier, thanks to a proliferation of gluten-free brands. I enlisted friends all over the country to help me search for the items used in the book. They scoured their neighborhood markets, big chain groceries, co-ops, and international markets and told me what they found—and what they didn't. The key below lists three different places to find ingredients. I use the key with each entry, indicating availability for that item. Regional differences may apply, but if your local stores lack the products you need, ask for them. Grocery stores are very receptive to customer requests. If all else fails, almost everything is available online (see Mail Order Sources, page 192).

KEY Grocery stores (G): This is your everyday grocery store. Many of the (non-refrigerated) ingredients can be found in an "Asian" or "international" aisle. Some grocery stores have a separate section dedicated to natural food and organics and this is where you may find gluten-free versions of more common ingredients, such as soy sauce, as well as many of the specialty flours.

Natural foods markets and upscale grocers (N): This category includes large, upscale markets such as Whole Foods and smaller, independent co-ops. Many of the co-ops have fewer overall choices, but you're more likely to find the gluten-free brands.

Asian or international markets (A): While some cities have Asian-specific markets, others have international food markets, covering flavors from around the globe. You can find most of what you need here, though I would be careful about purchasing any ingredient with questionable gluten content if it has a non-English label.

Asterisk (*): These ingredients can often contain gluten—be sure to check the label.

Produce/Refrigerated

These items will likely be found in the produce section or in another refrigerated case.

Bean sprouts (G, N, A): The two most commonly available types of bean sprouts are mung (often labeled "conventional") and soy bean sprouts. Mung bean sprouts are slender and white; soy bean sprouts are slightly plumper with a yellow bean attached to the end. The recipes in this book were tested with mung bean sprouts, but you can use either variety. Bean sprouts are extremely perishable; buy ones that look fresh and crisp and use them within 2 days.

Chiles, fresh (G, N, A): I call for jalapeño chiles (red or green) exclusively in this book, primarily because of their easy availability. Their heat level can vary tremendously; taste before you add them to a dish and adjust the amount if needed. Sometimes I call for red jalapeños, but mostly for visual purposes; you are welcome to use green chiles instead. If you are familiar with other types of chiles and can procure them in your area, substitute as you see fit.

Citrus fruit (G, N, A): Lemon or lime juice always means freshly squeezed. In some instances, the grated peel (zest) is used as well. If you have a glut of fresh citrus juice, freeze some in ice-cube trays and then store the cubes in resealable freezer bags for later.

Cucumber, English (G, N, A): A long, narrow, plastic-wrapped cucumber, less seedy and bitter and with thinner skin than its garden-variety cousin. The recipe will direct you whether or not to remove the peel and seeds.

Galangal (N): Also called Siamese ginger. Used for flavoring soups and curries, this rhizome tastes like a more pungent and citrusy version of ginger. Substitute with regular ginger in a pinch.

Garlic (G, N, A): Always use fresh garlic. Never buy prechopped garlic—it usually contains additives—but peeled garlic cloves from an Asian market make a great time-saving cheat. Store peeled garlic cloves in a covered container in the refrigerator.

Ginger, fresh (G, N, A): Choose a piece of ginger with smooth, thin skin. It should feel firm and heavy, not at all shriveled. Remove the skin with a paring knife or scrape it off with the tip of a spoon. The recipes specify many different ways to prepare ginger: grated, minced, chopped, or sliced. The cutting method makes a difference: grated ginger produces ginger juice, an important component in certain recipes; sliced ginger adds flavor but is removed before serving. Use the technique indicated in the recipe. Fresh ginger freezes well in a resealable freezer bag for up to 2 months. Break off pieces as needed.

Ginger, pickled* (N, A): Slices of fresh ginger pickled in vinegar and sugar. Some commercial brands contain so many additives it may be worthwhile to make your own batch (see page 35). Not all pickled ginger is sold refrigerated; some may be stocked alongside the Asian condiments.

Green onions (G, N, A): Also known as scallions. Trim the root end and about 2 inches off the green tops. The entire remainder is edible, but often divided and added at different times in a recipe. Cook the white and lighter green parts like an onion and add the darker green tops near the end like an herb.

Herbs, fresh (cilantro, mint, basil—G, N, A; Thai basil—A only): Fresh herbs are important flavor boosters in Asian cooking, but substitutions are possible (and listed) in many of the recipes. Thai basil has an anise flavor only vaguely similar to Italian basil that adds an intriguing flavor to stir-fries.

Kaffir lime leaves (N, A): Lime leaves provide possibly one of the most seductive aromas around and they are worth seeking out. The leaves from kaffir lime trees are used to flavor soups and curries and then removed before eating. They are available frozen and dried, but the fresh ones are the most aromatic. Find them packaged in plastic containers near the fresh herbs, or substitute lime zest. They may just be referred to as "lime leaves."

Kimchi* (some G, N, A): While the term kimchi can be used to refer to many varieties of pickled vegetables, in this book I specifically mean spicy Korean pickled cabbage. Sometimes kimchi is thickened with a wheat-flour paste; keep an eye out for that. If kimchi is not available in your area, try your hand at the Cabbage Kimchi recipe in this book (page 116).

Lemongrass (some G, N, A): Long and woody with the scent of citronella; it adds lemon flavor without the acidity of lemon juice. Lemongrass is very fibrous; first cut off all but the bottom 4 or 5 inches. Peel off the outer layers until you reach a tender white inner core. Use the core in one large chunk, smashing it first with the side of your knife to release its flavors. Add it to soups or chop it fine for curry pastes and marinades. Lemongrass freezes well. Look for it in the produce section in long (12 inches or more) grassy stems, or trimmed down and sold in plastic containers near the fresh herbs. Or you can substitute lemon zest.

Miso paste* (white, red, yellow) (G, N, A): Fermented soybean paste. Flavors can range from sweet and mild to salty and pungent; usually the darker colors have a stronger flavor. The most commonly available miso pastes are made from a combination of rice and soybeans, but some types use barley (mugi miso) or other grains. Be sure to use one based on gluten-free grains. White miso, also called shiro miso, is a sweet, light variety great for delicate marinades. Yellow miso, a slightly saltier type, is my everyday all-purpose miso. Red miso, considerably darker in color and bolder in flavor, makes perfect miso soup or mix several types together to form your own blend.

You can find miso refrigerated in small plastic tubs or sturdy bags. Occasionally in grocery stores you'll find it in an aseptic pack in the Asian-foods aisle or the organics aisle. Keep yours in the refrigerator for up to 6 months. Miso paste is the key ingredient in miso soup as well as a flavorful addition to sauces, marinades, and dressings.

Radish, daikon (N, A): Look for large, white Japanese radishes with smooth skin and a firm texture. Their crisp flesh can be grated as a condiment, braised in stews, or steamed in radish cakes.

Rice cakes (A): Also called rice sticks or dduk, a combination of rice flour and water formed into 3-inch-long cylinders or sliced flat ovals. Their chewy texture is a welcome addition to stir-fries or soups. You may find these frozen instead of refrigerated. Soak rice cakes in cold water for about an hour before cooking them.

Tofu (G, N, A): Also called bean curd; coagulated soy milk formed into a high-protein cake. Tofu is creamy white with a faint beany smell and mild flavor. Textures range from firm (best for cubes or sautéing) to silken (great for pureeing). Once you open the package, store any unused tofu submerged in fresh water, refrigerated, for just a few days. Many recipes suggest draining tofu before using it to remove excess water. To do this, set cubed tofu on a paper towel–lined plate for several minutes. Turn the tofu at least once, changing the towels if they get too wet. Tofu is usually sold in the refrigerated section (regular or organics area), or sometimes in an aseptic pack in the Asian condiments aisle.

Condiments, Sauces, and Pantry Items

Most of the sauces are found with the Asian condiments or in an organics or natural foods section unless otherwise indicated. Some items may also be in a general condiments aisle, near the ketchup or vinegar.

Bamboo shoots, canned (G, N, A): The tender, edible shoot of the bamboo plant. I call for canned bamboo shoots; drain and rinse them before using.

Bonito flakes (N, A): Shavings of dried bonito fish (similar to tuna), a key ingredient in dashi (page 36), Japanese sea stock. Bonito flakes have a mysterious smoky flavor. They're sold in bags alongside the Asian ingredients in natural food stores or near the dried sea vegetables in Asian markets.

Chicken broth* (G, N, A): Many commercial brands of chicken broth contain gluten. Make your own chicken broth (page 37) or look for one of the gluten-free brands in the soup aisle.

Chili-garlic sauce* (G, N, A): A coarse mixture of chiles, garlic, salt, and vinegar. Or try Sriracha, a smooth puree of similar ingredients. Use these sauces in recipes or at the table for an added bit of heat. Huy Fong brand is my favorite.

Chinese chile bean sauce* (N, A): Also called chile bean paste. At its most basic, this sauce is a combination of chiles and ground soybeans or black beans, salt, and oil. I like Lian How brand. You can make a substitute for $1^1/_2$ tablespoons chile bean sauce by combining 1 tablespoon miso paste with $1^1/_2$ teaspoons Sriracha sauce. For larger quantities, use 2 parts miso to 1 part Sriracha.

Coconut milk (G, N, A): For the recipes in this book, use unsweetened coconut milk, not cream of coconut. I often call for 14-ounce cans, but sizes range from 13.5 to 14.5 ounces; any of these are fine. In the can, the clear liquid sometimes separates to the bottom while the thick cream rises to the top. In some cases a recipe will call to spoon off the cream first and simmer it with curry paste; other times, you should stir the two together before cooking.

Curry paste* (G, N, A): Thai curry pastes include a variety of highly flavorful aromatics, often including chiles, shallots, lemongrass, garlic, galangal, fresh herbs, and spices. Curry paste is widely available, but the flavor of homemade curry paste (see page 33) is unsurpassed. Refrigerate after opening.

Fish sauce (G, N, A): Also called *nuoc mam* or *nam pla*. This clear, tea-colored brew comes from collecting the liquid as it drains from salted anchovies. It adds salt and savory richness to many Asian dishes. Fish sauce should be gluten-free, but do check the label for additives just to be safe. Refrigerate after opening.

Hoisin sauce* (some G, N, A): A brown, thick sauce based on fermented soybeans, garlic, sugar, spices, and often wheat flour. It lends sweetness and depth to a recipe. Look for one thickened with cornstarch or tapioca. Refrigerate after opening.

Kecap manis* (A): Sweet, thick soy sauce. Gluten-free brands are hard to find, but you can make your own: Simmer equal parts brown sugar and gluten-free soy sauce in a pan until the sugar dissolves, about 1 minute. Cool before using. I usually make a batch using $1/4$ cup of each and keep it in the refrigerator, covered, for up to 2 months.

Kombu (N, A): Dried kelp sheets, one of the key ingredients in dashi (page 36). The rectangular sheets are dark green, almost black in color. Break off the amount you need. Find kombu with the Asian ingredients in natural food stores or with the dried sea vegetables in Asian markets.

Mirin (G, N, A): A sweet, almost syrupy cooking wine brewed from glutinous rice (glutinous rice does not contain gluten), used in many marinades, sauces, and glazes. Because it's for cooking, not drinking, look for it with the Asian condiments. I prefer Takara brand. Mirin (used more for sweetening), rice vinegar (vinegar), and sake (an alcoholic beverage) are not at all substitutes for one another. In a pinch you can make a substitute for mirin by combining 1 cup sake and $1/2$ cup sugar in a small saucepan. Heat until the sugar dissolves. Cool before using. Keep any extra mirin, refrigerated, up to several months.

Mung beans, dried split (N, A): Purchase split yellow mung beans, also called "hulled" or "peeled" mung beans or *moong dal*. They will look similar to yellow split peas. Do not purchase dried whole green mung beans; these cook differently from the hulled beans. Because mung beans are commonly used in Indian and Middle Eastern cooking, you can find them in international markets or the bean section of natural food stores or well-stocked groceries. They must be soaked before cooking or pureeing.

Nori (N, A): Also called laver; a type of sea vegetable, most commonly used in dried sheets for wrapping sushi rolls. You can buy containers of finely shredded roasted nori to use as a topping, or cut nori sheets into fine strips with scissors. Look for unseasoned nori strips with the Asian ingredients in natural foods stores or with the sea vegetables in Asian markets.

Oil, cooking (G, N, A): For sautéing and stir-frying, I use vegetable oil or an organic canola oil refined for high-heat cooking. I avoid peanut oil due to allergy potential, but its high smoke point does make it an excellent option. Do not use olive oil because the flavor is too strong.

Oyster sauce* (some G, N, A): A thick, brown savory sauce made from oyster extracts, sugar, and salt. Choose the brand with the fewest ingredients, and one thickened with cornstarch instead of wheat flour. Refrigerate after opening.

Rice vinegar (G, N, A): Sometimes called rice wine vinegar; a mild low acidity vinegar made from rice. Do not use seasoned rice vinegar, which includes sugar, salt, and, often, high fructose corn syrup and MSG. (I call for "unseasoned rice vinegar" to differentiate it from the seasoned kind. The label will most likely just read "rice vinegar.") Rice vinegar, mirin, and sake are not interchangeable ingredients. I like Marukan organic rice vinegar, made from just water and rice, which may be found with other Asian condiments or in the vinegar section. Do check the label for additives just to be safe.

Salt (G, N, A): The recipes in this book were developed using Diamond Crystal kosher salt. Some other brands taste "saltier." Adjust the quantity as needed.

Sesame oil (G, N, A): Oil pressed from toasted sesame seeds. It is used as a flavoring in small amounts, not as a cooking oil for sautéing or stir-frying. Choose a golden-brown pure sesame oil in a small glass bottle. (I call for toasted sesame oil, as indicated by the dark color. The label may not say toasted.) Sesame oil is prone to rancidity, so once it's open store it in a cool pantry for up to a few months or longer in the refrigerator. If refrigerated, it will need to come to room temperature before measuring it. In the grocery store, it will be shelved with other Asian condiments, or possibly with the oils. I always use Kadoya brand.

Shiitake mushrooms, dried (N, A): A flavorful dried mushroom that needs to be soaked in warm water to rehydrate before cooking. You may find whole shiitake caps in Asian markets, which should be sliced after soaking, or presliced shiitakes in regular groceries. The flavor of dried shiitake is highly cocentrated and not interchangeable with fresh shiitake.

Soy sauce* (some G, N, A): Traditionally brewed from a combination of soybeans and wheat. Gluten-free options are available (also see Tamari). High-quality gluten-free soy sauce should contain very few ingredients. Look for brands containing water, soybeans, salt, and little else. Gluten-free brands may be found along with the other Asian condiments or in an organics aisle. You can purchase single-serving packets (see Mail Order Sources, page 192) to keep with you for restaurant emergencies.

Sriracha (some G, N, A): See Chili-garlic sauce.

Tahini (G, N, A): A paste made from ground sesame seeds. Asian versions of sesame paste are different (the seeds are toasted), but I use tahini in these recipes because it's so much easier to find. Look for it alongside the peanut butter or in the international aisle of the grocery store.

Tamari* (some G, N, A): A dark, rich soy sauce brewed with or without wheat. There are many brands of gluten-free tamari (see also Soy sauce), but read the label because not all tamari is wheat free. High-quality tamari should contain very few ingredients. Look for brands containing water, soybeans, salt, and little else, either with the Asian condiments or in the organics aisle. I use San-J gluten-free tamari. You can purchase single-serving packets (see Mail Order Sources, page 192) to keep with you for restaurant emergencies.

Teriyaki sauce* (some G, N, A): A thick, sweet, soy sauce–based sauce used for marinades and glazes. Some brands are gluten free or you can make your own; see page 26.

Wood ear (A): Also called black fungus or tree ear. This mushroom is more about adding texture than flavor to a dish. Soak the dried wood ear in hot water for about 15 minutes. Drain and rinse it and then prepare as directed; it will have a gelatinous, yet relatively firm texture. Find it in Asian markets near the dried mushrooms.

Spices

Single-ingredient spices are inherently gluten free, but spice blends or mixes can contain gluten. Read the label. McCormick does a great job of labeling ingredients containing wheat in bold letters. The spices below are found along with the other spices (often in the baking aisle) or with the Asian ingredients.

Chinese five-spice powder (some G, N, A): A blend of several spices, including star anise, Sichuan peppercorns, cinnamon, fennel, clove, or ginger. The flavor can be overwhelming; use it sparingly.

Korean chili powder (A): Dried Korean chiles, ground to a powder. The taste is hot and sweet with a hint of bitterness. The powder is available in a fine grind (often called red pepper powder) for cooking or a coarser grind for making kimchi. Because finding this spice requires a trip to an Asian market, you can substitute paprika with a pinch of cayenne pepper for the fine chili powder. For larger quantities, use about $1/4$ teaspoon of cayenne per tablespoon of paprika. If you're making kimchi, though, you should locate the coarse ground chili powder.

Sesame seeds (G, N, A): White sesame seeds, either plain or toasted. You can buy containers of pre-toasted sesame seeds in Asian markets, or just toast them in a small dry skillet over medium heat until light brown. Look for sesame seeds in the spice aisle, or near the Asian condiments. I store mine in the refrigerator to prevent rancidity.

Shichimi togarashi (N, A): A beguiling Japanese spice blend including such flavor boosters as dried chiles, sesame seeds, dried citrus peel, and nori. Look for it with the spices or Asian condiments. Do not mistake it for *togarashi*, which is just dried chile pepper.

Star anise (N, A): A star-shaped dried pod used to flavor soups and braised dishes with a hint of licorice.

Flours/Starches/Baking

Most of these items can be found in the baking aisle of grocery stores or in the natural foods or organics aisle. Thai flours are available at Asian markets.

Almond meal (some G, N): Blanched almonds ground into a fine flour.

Cornstarch (G, N, A): Used in many Asian preparations as a thickener, binder, and coating for fried foods. It also lends chewiness when combined with other flours in doughs and batters. Check the label for additives to confirm it's gluten-free.

Millet flour (some G, N): Ground from whole-grain millet. An excellent high-protein flour.

Oats, gluten-free rolled* (some G, N): Be sure to purchase a brand of certified gluten-free oats. I use Bob's Red Mill.

Potato starch (N, A): Used here as a thickener and for dredging food before sautéing. Do not confuse it with potato flour; they are not the same.

Sweet rice flour (some G, N, A; Thai flour, A only): Flour ground from grains of sticky (sweet) rice. I like Koda Farms Mochiko Blue Star brand, but there are other American and Thai brands available. Do not confuse sweet rice flour with white rice flour; they have completely different properties and yield entirely different results.

Tapioca flour (some G, N, A): Also called tapioca starch; derived from cassava (manioc) root. Tapioca makes a great gluten-free thickener and crisp coating for fried foods, and also adds translucency and resilience to dumpling dough. Tapioca flour is often an ingredient in rice paper wrappers.

White rice flour (some G, N, A; Thai flour, A only): Flour ground from long-grain rice. Thai brands of rice flour are more finely ground and less grainy than American rice flours, resulting in a smoother-textured final product. You can usually use either type, but I will specify in a recipe if using a Thai brand is essential. My favorite is Erawan Thai white rice flour. Do not confuse white rice flour with sweet rice flour; they have completely different properties and yield entirely different results.

Xanthan gum (N): A powdered additive used as a thickener or to add pliability and structure to gluten-free baked goods. It is produced through the bacterial fermentation of sugar, usually corn.

Rice

In Asian markets rice has a dedicated aisle; in regular groceries, look for rice alongside the Asian ingredients, in the organics aisle, or near the rice and pasta. For detailed information on rice, see page 98.

Jasmine rice (G, N, A): A long-grain, aromatic rice predominantly used in Thai and Vietnamese cooking. Once cooked, the grains remain distinct.

Rice paper wrapper (some G, N, A): Also called spring roll wrappers or spring roll skins; thin brittle rounds made from rice flour, or a combination of rice and tapioca flour, and water. They must be soaked in water to rehydrate before wrapping them around fillings.

Sticky rice (N, A): Also called sweet rice or glutinous rice. Sticky rice does not contain gluten; *glutinous* refers to its sticky texture. It is available in either long or short grain and can be used in both sweet and savory preparations. Sticky rice must be soaked for several hours before cooking.

Sushi rice (N, A): Some packages are labeled *sushi rice*; otherwise, you can use a Japanese-style medium- or short-grain rice. These shorter grains of rice clump together when cooked. When preparing sushi, mix the cooked rice with vinegar, sugar, and salt (see Sushi Rice, page 100).

Noodles

Noodles have a dedicated aisle in Asian markets. In regular groceries, look for noodles alongside the Asian ingredients or in the pasta or organics aisles. Avoid all noodles containing wheat, such as ramen, somen, egg noodles, udon, and more. In all cases, be sure to read the labels. For detailed information on noodles, see page 80.

Cellophane noodles (some G, N, A): Also called mung bean noodles, glass noodles, bean threads, *sai fun,* or *harasume;* noodles made from the starch of mung beans. The thin white noodles become transparent once they are cooked. Soak them in warm water for 15 minutes before using them in a recipe.

Rice noodles (G, N, A): Noodles made from rice flour and water. They come in many shapes and sizes; look at the noodle itself as well as the name on the package to determine what you need. Rice vermicelli, the thinnest, needs only a soak in boiling water to cook. Thicker flat rice noodles, often called rice sticks, are generally precooked in boiling water and then reheated quickly in a stir-fry or soup. Watch out for fresh rice noodles, which sometimes contain wheat starch.

Soba noodles* (N, A): Soba noodles are made from buckwheat flour (a gluten-free grain), but many versions contain wheat flour as well. Use only 100 percent buckwheat soba. Soba noodles need no preliminary soaking; boil them and then rinse off the extra starch before serving or stir-frying.

Alcohol

For the most successful results, use only sake and wine in your cooking that is good enough to drink. These items can be purchased from your grocery store, but be sure to buy them from the wine section; cooking wines found in the condiment aisle are very low quality and generally have plenty of additives, including salt. Asian markets will have the largest selection of sake and rice wine. *Please note:* Sake and rice wine are not interchangeable with rice vinegar (even if it is labeled *rice wine vinegar*, it's still vinegar) or mirin, which is used more as a sweetener. If you don't have a wheat-free Shaoxing rice wine (a rice wine used in many of the recipes), a medium-dry sherry makes a good substitute.

Dry sherry (some G, N, wine stores): Although sherry is not an Asian ingredient, a nutty, rich, medium-dry sherry—such as amontillado or oloroso—makes a reasonable substitute for Shaoxing wine. Do not use cooking sherry, which is generally very poor quality and contains additives.

Sake (some G, N, A, wine stores): An alcoholic beverage brewed from polished rice. Sake is naturally gluten free. It comes in many styles, but for cooking you can choose a crisp, dry inexpensive sake. If you're not a sake drinker, some stores sell small (180 ml) bottles, perfect to have on hand for your cooking needs. For more detailed information on sake, see page 176.

Shaoxing rice wine* (N, A): Rich and smooth, made from glutinous rice (which is gluten free) and water. The wine can occasionally contain wheat; look for a brand without wheat or substitute a medium-dry sherry.

Umeshu (some G, N, A): Also called plum wine; made from steeping *ume* (a Japanese fruit similar to plums) in distilled alcohol and sugar. Great as a light aperitif or in Plum Wine Sangria (page 181). Plum wine is often shelved right next to the sake.

Be sure to use only gluten-free brands.

The Short List

Many sauces and marinades rely on different combinations of the same basic Asian ingredients. These ingredients show up over and over again throughout the book. It's worth stocking your pantry with these common essentials so that you can limit last-minute shopping trips to a quick stop for fresh produce, meat, and fish.

TOP TEN SPECIALTY ITEMS	COMMONLY USED PRODUCE	PANTRY ITEMS
Soy sauce* or tamari*	Garlic	Chicken broth*
Toasted sesame oil	Ginger	Cornstarch
Asian fish sauce	Green onions	Red pepper flakes
Unseasoned rice vinegar	Jalapeño chiles	Rice (jasmine, medium grain)
Sake	Limes	Sesame seeds
Coconut milk		Sugar
Mirin		Tapioca flour
Sriracha sauce (or other chili-garlic sauce*)		Vegetable oil
Miso paste* (white or yellow)		White rice flour
Noodles: rice, cellophane, or 100% buckwheat soba		

*Be sure to use only gluten-free brands.

Tools and Techniques

Listed below are some of the tools I use throughout the book. This does not mean you need to buy them; I simply want to introduce you to some items that can lighten your workload considerably. Realistically, you can prepare all of the recipes in this book with a few sharp knives, a basic set of pots and pans, a pair of tongs, and a spatula or two.

One tool that warrants separate mention is the recipe itself. In order to use a recipe to its fullest potential, be sure to read the whole thing through before starting to cook. You don't want to discover any surprises midway through dinner preparation. The Heads Up box attempts to alert you to potential diversions, such as subrecipes, lengthy marinating, or chilling times. Reading the whole recipe arms you with all the relevant information to create a successful dish.

Pots and Pans

Dutch oven: A heavy casserole that can withstand stove-top simmering. It's great for braised dishes and curries. A large pot (about 6-quart capacity) with a lid is an appropriate substitute.

Frying pan or skillet: For sautéing and stir-frying. A medium frying pan (8 to 10 inches) is useful for many tasks, but if you plan to stir-fry in a pan instead of a wok, it is important to have a large pan as well, measuring at least 12 inches, preferably 14 inches.

Nonstick frying pan: For cooking pancakes, dumplings, and other potentially sticky foods. Keep a medium (8 to 10 inches) and large (12 inches) nonstick pan with a lid on hand. If you don't have a lid, create a makeshift version with a round pizza pan or similarly shaped item.

Saucepans and pots: For simmering sauces, boiling noodles, and making soups and braised dishes. I refer to the following approximate sizes in the recipes—small (2 quart), medium (4 quart), large (6 to 8 quart), stockpot (12 quart or larger).

Steamer: You can purchase a steamer or make one in a pot you already own. Purchase either a stackable metal or bamboo steamer with at least two perforated trays for holding food and a lid to cover the top tray. These steamers can rest over boiling water in your wok or a regular pot.

You can also craft a steamer in a regular pot or a wok. I put a small round metal rack in the bottom of my wok or a wide, deep pot. I put the items to be steamed on a small, lightly oiled plate and set the plate on the rack over simmering water, without touching the water. You can also use an empty can as a pedestal to hold the plate above the water level or scrunch a piece of foil into a long snake shape, bring the ends together to form a ring, then set the plate on top. Continually check the water level and add more as needed. You will need to cover the wok (or pot) with a lid during steaming.

Wok: As long as you have a large (preferably 14-inch) frying pan, you do not absolutely need a wok. But they are really fun to use and can be used for deep frying and steaming as well. You can even make soup in the wok. If you decide to take the plunge, look for a carbon steel wok, about 14 inches in diameter. I prefer the type with a rounded bottom that sits on a stabilizing wok ring right atop the stove flame. If you have an electric stove, you should probably choose a flat-bottom wok. Do not buy a nonstick wok or something fancy and expensive. In fact, a good wok should run you less than $30 at an Asian market. (Or order one from The Wok Shop; see Mail Order Sources, page 192.) If you plan to use your wok for steaming or smoking, pick up a lid as well; otherwise, you don't really need one.

A carbon steel wok requires a bit of care to keep it in proper working order. When you first bring it home, you need to season it. Wash the wok with dish soap and warm water to remove any factory grease. Dry it well and then lightly coat the wok inside and out with oil—vegetable or peanut oil is fine. Cover any nonremovable handles with aluminum foil and then put the wok in a 425°F oven for 20 minutes. Remove the wok from the oven with pot holders and let any remaining oil cool before wiping the wok dry with paper towels. Now you're ready to cook. From this point on, clean your wok only with warm water and a firm, nonmetallic scrubber, but no soap. Dry the wok completely over a low flame to prevent rust.

Other Helpful Gadgets

Benriner slicer: Also known as a Japanese mandoline. If you like perfectly sliced vegetables or evenly shredded carrots, this is an inexpensive way to attain uniformity.

Chinese wire mesh strainer: A web of wire mesh attached to a long bamboo handle. Ideal tool for lifting dumplings from boiling water or fried foods from hot oil. Or use a large, long-handled slotted spoon instead. I use mine all the time.

Dowel or small rolling pin: For rolling dumpling dough.

Ginger grater: If I had to pick one single item from this list for you to purchase, this would be it. They are small, inexpensive, and the absolute easiest way to grate ginger. My favorites are ceramic or porcelain graters with a raised lip around the edge for holding in the ginger juice. A regular box grater will not effectively grate ginger, but you could use a microplane grater instead.

Grill grate: A nonstick or stainless steel grid. Put it on top of the grill grates to keep fish from sticking or smaller pieces of vegetables from falling through the gaps.

Rice cooker: A mainstay in Asian kitchens, rice cookers produce foolproof rice at the press of a button. It may be worth considering if you eat a lot of rice and would rather not have to think about cooking it.

Scale: I don't know how anyone lives without a kitchen scale, but then again I'm a recipe developer. There are very few recipes in this book that call specifically for a weight measurement of produce. If you don't own a scale, weigh what you need on one of the scales in the produce department of the grocery store.

Scissors: I keep a special pair of kitchen scissors for snipping fresh herbs and cutting unwieldy noodles into smaller lengths.

Skewers: Disposable bamboo skewers or metal skewers for spearing meat, chicken, fish, and vegetables.

Thermometer: Another very inexpensive but useful item. Use a candy or deep-fry thermometer to monitor the oil temperature in deep-frying recipes.

Wok spatula: A long-handled curved metal spatula, almost resembling a shovel. You could use a wooden spoon or large long-handled metal spoon instead.

Techniques

Deep-frying: Heat about $2^1/_2$ to 3 inches of vegetable oil over medium heat to the temperature noted in the recipe. You can do this in a wok or a large saucepan. Gauge the temperature with a deep-fry thermometer, or sprinkle a drop of water in the oil. When it sizzles vigorously, you're ready to cook. Do not crowd the pan. Stir or turn the food occasionally to keep it from sticking together. When the first batch is done, remove the food with a slotted spoon or a Chinese mesh strainer and transfer it to a rack or a paper towel–lined plate. Season it immediately, while it's hot. Make sure the oil returns to the proper cooking temperature before adding the next batch. When the oil cools completely, you can strain it into the original container and reuse it one or two times.

Rolling rice paper wrappers: Rice paper wrappers must be rehydrated before forming them into rolls. For salad rolls, soak two rice paper wrappers at a time in warm water until pliable, about 30 seconds. Carefully remove the wrappers and set them on a clean kitchen towel. For rolling instructions, see the photos on page 52. Transfer the finished rolls to a platter and cover with a damp paper towel. Repeat with the remaining wrappers and filling. The rolls can be assembled several hours ahead. Cover them with a damp paper towel and then plastic wrap, and refrigerate.

Steaming: Fill a wok or a large pot with several inches of water (the water should not touch the bottom of the steamer or the plate). Line the tray of a metal or bamboo steamer basket with parchment paper or lettuce leaves to keep the food from sticking. Bring the water to a boil. Steam the food, covered, as directed. Check the water level occasionally and refresh as necessary to keep the pan from running dry.

Stir-frying: The key to successful stir-frying is having all your ingredients chopped and measured before you begin cooking. (Sometimes I do this earlier in the day and keep the whole tray in the refrigerator until it's time to cook.) When you're ready to stir-fry, heat the wok or a large (14-inch) frying pan over medium-high to high heat. When the pan is hot, add the oil. When the oil starts to shimmer, add the ingredients in the order indicated, and keep them moving in the pan. If your pan is too small, cook the recipe in two batches. Likewise, if you want to double any of the recipes, cook them in two batches. A crowded pan will cause the food to steam, not sear, resulting in a very different and much less appetizing dish.

TWO Sauces and Stocks

Many cookbooks relegate sauces to merely a supporting role, almost an afterthought, but I'm inclined to put them front and center. Sauces play not only a critical role as purveyors of flavor, but also have the ability to undermine a gluten-free diet. It only takes a drop of regular soy sauce to tarnish an otherwise safe dish. Once you identify what makes many of the traditional Asian sauces off-limits (see Identifying Sources of Gluten in Common Asian Ingredients, page 6), it is often possible to recreate them in a gluten-free way. And for those you can't replicate at home, don't fret. More and more companies are recognizing the demand for gluten-free Asian basics; new products appear with promising frequency. Use your buying power to ask for what you need. At the very least, every single supermarket should carry a gluten-free soy sauce or tamari. If yours does not, ask for it and then ask again (and again) until you see it on the shelf.

Gluten-free issues aside, many Asian sauces ingeniously combine sweet (sugar, honey), tart (citrus juices, vinegar), salty (fish sauce, soy sauce), and spicy (fresh chiles, dried chiles) ingredients to keep flavors balanced in the final dish. As the cook, you have the freedom to tweak the sauces, personalizing them to your taste buds. Sample the sauce as you go, adding a touch more sugar or a few less chiles to make it your own. (This is especially important with the spicy ingredients. Even the heat in innocent jalapeños can range from benign to burning.) When tasting, keep in mind the sauce should taste somewhat bold on its own because it will be muted when combined with the other components.

From a practical standpoint, keeping a few of these sauces in the refrigerator at all times greatly enhances your ability to get dinner on the table fast. All of them can be made in advance, anywhere from several days to two weeks. If you wind up with extra sauce or you want to double down, each sauce recipe mentions all the places in the book where it can be used. But don't limit yourself; get to know these sauces and then use them to dress up the most basic weeknight dinners, from grilled chicken breasts to a vegetable stir-fry with steamed rice. Their versatility will serve you well.

Soy Vinegar Dipping Sauce

 MAKES ABOUT ½ CUP

I like a little chile heat to balance the flavors in this potent sauce, but complete control of the spiciness rests in your hands. Experiment with fresh chiles versus dried to see how they affect the flavor. If you have any extra sauce, drizzle it over steamed rice.

¼ **cup soy sauce or tamari** GF

3 tablespoons unseasoned rice vinegar

1½ teaspoons sugar

1 teaspoon toasted sesame oil

2–3 slices fresh jalapeño, or large pinch of red pepper flakes (optional)

Stir together all the ingredients in a small serving bowl. The dipping sauce will keep, covered, in the refrigerator for about 1 week with fresh jalapeño or 2 weeks with red pepper flakes.

USES FOR SOY VINEGAR DIPPING SAUCE
Porcupine Balls (page 48)
Gingery Pork Pot Stickers (page 58)
Korean Green Onion Pancakes (page 70)

Teriyaki Sauce

 MAKES ABOUT ¾ CUP

In addition to a laundry list of other ingredients, most commercial brands of teriyaki sauce contain gluten. Whip up this tastier homemade version in just minutes.

½ **cup mirin**

¼ **cup soy sauce or tamari** GF

2 tablespoons honey

2 thin slices unpeeled fresh ginger

1 clove garlic, smashed

Pinch of red pepper flakes

In a small saucepan, combine the mirin, soy sauce, honey, ginger, garlic, and red pepper flakes. Bring to a boil. Lower the heat and simmer until thickened, about 10 minutes. Remove the ginger and garlic. The sauce will keep, covered, in the refrigerator for about 2 weeks.

USES FOR TERIYAKI SAUCE
Chicken and Vegetable Yakitori (page 40)
Sesame-Crusted Salmon (page 137)

Nuoc Cham

 MAKES ABOUT 1³/₄ CUPS

Nuoc cham is a staple of the Vietnamese table and enhances recipes throughout this book. The sauce is very basic, yet it introduces a balance of sweet, tart, salty, and spicy to your meal. Keep a batch in the fridge for up to 2 weeks.

¹/₃ cup sugar

1 cup very warm tap water

¹/₄ cup Asian fish sauce

1 tablespoon freshly squeezed lime juice

1 tablespoon unseasoned rice vinegar

1 clove garlic, minced

¹/₄ teaspoon red pepper flakes

In a small bowl, combine the sugar with the water. Stir until the sugar dissolves. Add the fish sauce, lime juice, rice vinegar, garlic, and red pepper flakes. Refrigerate until ready to use. The sauce will keep, covered, in the refrigerator for about 2 weeks.

USES FOR NUOC CHAM
Lemongrass Shrimp Skewers (page 44)
Roasted Pork Meatballs (page 47)
Crispy Spring Rolls (page 52)
Sticky Rice Dumplings with Chicken and Mushrooms (page 56)
Tapioca Dumplings with Beef and Shallots (page 62)
Vietnamese-Style Sizzling Rice Crepes (page 74)
Steamed Rice Sheets with Pork and Shrimp Filling (page 76)
Vietnamese Rice Noodle Salad (page 84)
Sautéed Catfish with Peanuts and Fresh Herbs (page 135)

Sweet Miso Glaze

 MAKES ABOUT 1⅓ CUPS

The huge selection of miso pastes available in Asian markets can be daunting for anyone, but you should have no trouble if you keep a few things in mind. Purchase miso that is based on a combination of soybeans and rice (stay away from any made from barley). For this recipe, look for the words "white," "sweet white," or "shiro miso" on the label; this is a sweeter and lighter variety. Darker versions are saltier with more intense flavors and may overwhelm the delicacy of the glaze.

½ cup sake

½ cup mirin

¼ cup sugar

1½ tablespoons grated fresh ginger

½ cup white miso (shiro miso) paste **GF**

In a small saucepan, bring the sake, mirin, sugar, and ginger to a simmer. Whisk in the miso paste and simmer gently until the sauce thickens, about 10 minutes. The sauce will keep, covered, in the refrigerator for 1 week.

USES FOR SWEET MISO GLAZE
Eggplant with Sweet Miso Glaze (page 123)

HEADS UP
You will need to chill the miso glaze completely before adding it to raw meat or fish.

Savory Miso Glaze

 MAKES ABOUT 1¼ CUPS

The previous recipe for sweet miso glaze is a delicate sauce that suits vegetables perfectly, but I wanted a bolder, saltier glaze for coating meat and fish. You can use the same type of miso paste in this recipe as in the sweeter version, just use a bit more of it here. I keep some of the glaze in the refrigerator at all times; it lasts for weeks and tastes great on a variety of proteins.

---

¹/₃ cup sake

¹/₃ cup mirin

¹/₄ cup sugar

²/₃ cup yellow or white miso paste **GF**

In a small saucepan, bring the sake, mirin, and sugar to a simmer. Whisk in the miso paste and simmer gently until the sauce is thick enough to coat a spoon, about 3 minutes. Cool the sauce completely before marinating fish or meat. The sauce will keep, covered, in the refrigerator for several weeks.

USES FOR SAVORY MISO GLAZE
Miso Glazed Scallops (page 45)
Black Cod Broiled with Savory Miso Glaze (page 136)

HEADS UP
You will need to chill the miso glaze completely before adding it to meat or fish.

Fiery Ginger Sauce

 MAKES ABOUT 1 CUP

While developing the recipe for Khao Man Gai (page 155), I discovered that this sauce tasted great on everything else I was cooking that day too. The flavor comes from lots of raw ginger—about ¹/₂ cup minced—and you'll want the pieces very finely chopped. A food processor makes quick work of the mincing, but if you don't have one, chop the ginger as finely as you can with a knife. And the garlic is also raw, so you may need to pass around breath mints for dessert. Try the sauce on grilled fish or steamed broccoli.

1 (2-ounce) piece peeled fresh ginger, cut into 6 pieces

6 cloves garlic

¹/₄ cup soy sauce or tamari GF

¹/₄ cup unseasoned rice vinegar

3 tablespoons sugar

2 tablespoons yellow or white miso paste GF

1 to 2 tablespoons minced red jalapeño chile

In a food processor, pulse the ginger until finely chopped, about ten (1-second) pulses. Scrape the ginger into a measuring cup; you should have almost ¹/₂ cup of chopped ginger. Return the ginger to the food processor and add the garlic. Process until both are finely chopped, about 20 seconds. (Alternatively, if you don't have a food processor, mince the ginger and garlic with a knife. You want the ginger very finely minced because you will be eating it raw.)

Add the soy sauce, rice vinegar, sugar, and miso paste to the food processor. Process until the ingredients are well combined, about 1 minute. Transfer the sauce to a small bowl and stir in the minced chile. The sauce will keep, covered, in the refrigerator for up to 3 days.

USES FOR FIERY GINGER SAUCE
Crispy Spring Rolls (page 52)
Shrimp and Sweet Potato Tempura Pancakes (page 72)
Salt and Pepper Squid (page 139)
Khao Man Gai (page 155)

Peanut Satay Sauce

 MAKES ABOUT 2 CUPS

Use this versatile peanut sauce not only as a dip for grilled satay skewers but also as the backbone for Stir-Fried Rice Noodles with Chicken and Peanut Sauce (page 83). The sauce contains a little bit of heat, but you can cut back on it or eliminate it altogether if you think it will scare the kids. The sauce keeps for days, but inevitably thickens as it sits. You can thin the sauce with a little coconut milk, water, or gluten-free chicken broth.

1/2 cup no-stir organic peanut butter

3 tablespoons soy sauce or tamari GF

1 tablespoon grated fresh ginger

1 tablespoon brown sugar

1 tablespoon mirin

2 teaspoons Sriracha or other chili-garlic sauce GF

1/2 teaspoon ground coriander

1 cup water

1 tablespoon freshly squeezed lime juice, more if needed

In a small saucepan, combine the peanut butter, soy sauce, ginger, brown sugar, mirin, Sriracha, and coriander. Stir in the water. Heat the ingredients over medium heat, stirring to combine. Do not let the sauce boil or it will separate. The consistency of the sauce should be pourable, but it will likely thicken as it sits. When the peanut sauce is hot, stir in the lime juice. Taste the sauce and add a little more lime juice if you like more acidity. The sauce will keep, covered, in the refrigerator for about 1 week.

VARIATION Use smooth or crunchy almond butter instead of peanut butter for a healthy and delicious alternative.

USES FOR PEANUT SATAY SAUCE
Grilled Pork Satay (page 42)
Halibut Satay with Thai Cucumber Relish (page 43)
Salad Rolls with Crab and Spicy Mango Sauce (page 51)
Stir-Fried Rice Noodles with Chicken and Peanut Sauce
    (page 83)

Spicy Mango Sauce

 MAKES ABOUT 1½ CUPS

Depending on the size and sweetness of your mango, you may have to adjust the vinegar and chiles to your taste. Don't be alarmed by green flecks in the sauce; once you puree the chiles and cilantro their color starts to take over.

1¼ cups diced fresh or frozen mango (thawed if frozen)

¼ cup loosely packed fresh cilantro leaves

2 tablespoons unseasoned rice vinegar

1 tablespoon grated fresh ginger

1 tablespoon vegetable oil

1 jalapeño chile, seeds and ribs removed

¾ teaspoon salt

Combine the mango, cilantro, vinegar, ginger, oil, jalapeño, and salt in a blender. Puree until smooth. The sauce will keep, covered, in the refrigerator for about 3 days.

> USES FOR SPICY MANGO SAUCE
> Roasted Pork Meatballs (page 47)
> Salad Rolls with Crab and Spicy Mango Sauce (page 51)

Super Secret Spicy Sauce

 MAKES ABOUT ½ CUP

Have you ever wondered how they make that crazy delicious sauce in a spicy tuna roll? Well this version comes close and it couldn't be easier. Use a dollop wherever you need a spicy kick; note the sauce gets spicier the longer it sits.

½ cup mayonnaise

2 tablespoons Sriracha sauce

In a small bowl, mix together the mayonnaise and the Sriracha. The sauce will keep, covered, in the refrigerator for up to 2 weeks.

> USES FOR SUPER SECRET SPICY SAUCE
> Sushi Rice Bowl (page 107)
> Salt and Pepper Squid (page 139)

Fresh Green Curry Paste

 MAKES ABOUT 1 CUP

I think this curry paste actually tastes green. It has a grassy, herbal quality to it, but it also packs some serious heat. I love mixing it with coconut milk as the base for a quick curry sauce. Because the jalapeño seeds are part of the sauce, taste the chiles before using them and cut back if they are excessively hot. I find it easiest to weigh the ingredients so you can just toss them in the food processor, but I've included quantity measures as well in case you don't have a scale. This paste freezes well, so you may want to double the batch and freeze it in 1/2-cup amounts.

2 or 3 jalapeño chiles (about 3 1/2 ounces), stems removed

2 shallots (about 3 ounces), peeled and coarsely chopped (about 1/2 cup)

4 cloves garlic

1 (1-ounce) piece fresh ginger, peeled and cut into 4 pieces (about 2 tablespoons coarsely chopped)

1 cup packed fresh cilantro leaves and stems

1 tablespoon Asian fish sauce

1 tablespoon grated fresh lime zest (from about 2 large limes)

1 1/2 teaspoons ground coriander

1/2 teaspoon ground cumin

1/4 teaspoon salt

Add the jalapeños, shallots, garlic, and ginger to the bowl of a food processor and pulse until finely chopped, about ten (1-second) pulses. Remove the lid and scrape down the sides of the bowl with a spatula.

Add the cilantro, fish sauce, lime zest, coriander, cumin, and salt. Process until the ingredients are well combined, stopping to scrape the bowl at least once, about 30 seconds. The curry paste will keep, covered, in the refrigerator for 2 days or freeze it for up to 2 months.

USES FOR FRESH GREEN CURRY PASTE
Rice Paper–Wrapped Salmon in Green Curry Sauce (page 138)
Green Curry Chicken (page 153)

Pickled Ginger

 MAKES ABOUT 1½ CUPS

In sushi restaurants, pickled ginger provides a zingy burst of acidity to the raw fish. I love how it counteracts the fattiness of certain types of fish, acting as a palate cleanser. You can certainly buy pickled ginger (after reading the label), but I prefer this simple version, free from preservatives and artificial coloring. Use the scale in the produce department to weigh the ginger if you don't have one at home.

8 ounces fresh ginger, peeled and cut into 2-inch lengths

1 cup unseasoned rice vinegar

⅓ cup sugar

1½ teaspoons salt

HEADS UP
You'll need to marinate the ginger for 24 hours before serving.

Bring a small saucepan of water to a boil. Cut the ginger lengthwise into paper-thin slices. Add the ginger to the water and cook for 30 seconds (you don't need to bring the water back to a boil). Drain the ginger in a colander and then transfer it to paper towels or a clean kitchen towel to dry. Transfer the ginger to a glass jar or other heatproof container with a lid.

In the same pan, combine the vinegar, sugar, and salt. Bring to a boil. Cook, stirring occasionally, until the sugar and salt dissolve, about 1 minute. Pour the hot liquid over the ginger and let it cool to room temperature. For best results, let the ginger marinate in the refrigerator for about a day before serving. The pickled ginger will keep, covered, in the refrigerator for about 2 weeks.

USES FOR PICKLED GINGER
Sushi Rice Bowl (page 107)
Black Cod Broiled with Savory Miso Glaze (page 136)

Dashi

 MAKES ABOUT 1 QUART

This Japanese sea stock is ridiculously quick and easy to prepare. Kombu, a type of dried kelp, comes in long rectangular or square pieces, almost black in color. I usually measure the size I need and break off a piece if it's too big. The surface of the kombu often bears a dusty coating of white powder, which is completely normal. Bonito flakes are shavings (they actually look like pencil shavings!) of dried bonito fish. Their smoky flavor lends a mysterious quality to the stock. Finding the two ingredients may be your only challenge, but they should be available in Asian markets, or natural food stores. You may find instant dashi powder there as well, but it often contains gluten. Besides, it's much tastier just to make it from scratch.

1 (5 by 4-inch) piece kombu (about $1/2$ ounce)

$4^{1}/2$ cups cold water

1 cup ($1/2$ ounce) packed bonito flakes

In a large saucepan, combine the kombu and the water. Let the kombu soak for 15 to 20 minutes. Bring the water just to a simmer over medium heat. Remove the kombu from the pan with tongs and discard it.

Lower the heat to low. Add the bonito flakes to the pan and stir. Cook for 5 minutes. Strain the dashi into a bowl through a fine-mesh strainer. The dashi will keep, covered, in the refrigerator for about 4 days, or freeze it for up to 1 month.

USES FOR DASHI
Greens in Smoky Dashi Broth (page 122)
Miso Broth with Steamed Clams (page 143)

Quick Miso Soup MAKES 1 CUP

1 cup dashi (above)

1 tablespoon miso paste GF

1 tablespoon minced green onion

Heat the dashi in a small saucepan. Whisk in the miso paste and cook the soup until hot, 2 to 3 minutes. Top with the green onion. If you want to include some tiny cubes of firm tofu, simmer them in the dashi for 1 to 2 minutes before adding the miso.

Chicken Broth

 MAKES ABOUT 3¹/₂ QUARTS

Here is a very basic broth recipe, good for Asian and non-Asian recipes alike. I make homemade chicken broth whenever I can (it freezes well), not only for the vast improvement in flavor over canned broth but also for the full-bodied mouthfeel. Since you discard the chicken pieces after making the broth, I use an inexpensive combination of wings, backs, and necks, resulting in both meaty flavor and a rich texture.

4 to 4¹/₂ pounds assorted chicken parts, such as wings, necks, and backs

4¹/₂ quarts (18 cups) water

1 large onion, coarsely chopped

1 tablespoon salt

Rinse the chicken pieces and then put them in a stockpot. Add the water and bring to a boil over medium-high heat. Let the water boil for about 1 minute and then lower the heat to a simmer. Skim and discard any foam that rises to the surface.

Add the onion to the pot. Simmer the broth over medium-low heat—the surface of the liquid should be bubbling very gently—for 1 hour. Add the salt and simmer for 1 hour longer. Remove the pot from the heat.

Using a slotted spoon, remove the chicken bones from the broth and discard them. To remove the fat from the broth, either strain the broth, in batches, through a fat separator, or strain the broth into a large bowl and refrigerate it overnight. Once the broth has chilled, the fat will congeal on the surface and you can remove it easily with a spoon. The chicken broth will keep, covered, in the refrigerator for up to 3 days, or freeze it in quart-size containers for several months.

THREE Skewers and Snacks

You can serve the recipes in this chapter as snacks, but an assortment of these versatile nibbles can work equally well as appetizers, as part of an enticing buffet, or elevated to main-dish status. Because most of the recipes include some make-ahead prep—leaving only the cooking for last minute—they're perfect for entertaining.

The chapter begins with an assortment of meat, seafood, and vegetable kebabs, each infused with flavor from a collection of gluten-free marinades and sauces. After the skewers, I turn my attention to a couple of unique meatballs, both very different from the breadcrumb-bound Italian and Swedish-style meatballs I used to enjoy. Here, as is often the case with Asian-influenced meatballs, cornstarch lightens the texture of the Roasted Pork Meatballs, and a beaten egg holds the Porcupine Balls together. And as a finale, rolled and wrapped treats. Rice paper wrappers, made from rice flour or a combination of rice flour and tapioca flour, make their first appearance as wraps for delightful crab-studded salad rolls and again for Crispy Spring Rolls. A savory Korean-style grilled chicken becomes an ideal "taco" filling, wrapped in warm Mandarin pancakes (page 68), corn tortillas, or rice paper.

For the most part, these recipes serve six as an appetizer or four as a main dish if you toss in a side dish or two. I usually count on 1 1/2 pounds of chicken, fish, or meat as a main dish for four, but if you have a pack of growing teenagers or especially robust eaters please adjust your output accordingly. And be sure to check out the Vietnamese Rice Noodle Salad (page 84), which offers the possibility of incorporating many of the recipes in this chapter into a unique one-dish meal.

Chicken and Vegetable Yakitori

SERVES 4 AS A MAIN DISH, 6 AS AN APPETIZER

With a batch of teriyaki sauce in the fridge, a quick family meal can be ready at a moment's notice. Grill the yakitori over medium heat so the sauce glazes and browns on the chicken without burning. I add a touch of orange zest to the remaining sauce for dipping, but you can leave it out if you prefer. If your family loves dipping, double the teriyaki sauce; you can always drizzle any extra over rice or save it for later.

1¹/₂ pounds boneless, skinless chicken thighs, cut into 1-inch cubes

6 green onions, white parts only, cut into ¹/₂-inch lengths

1 green bell pepper, cut into 1-inch dice

¹/₄ pound cremini mushrooms, wiped clean, halved or quartered if large

2 tablespoons vegetable oil, plus more for oiling the grill

¹/₂ teaspoon salt

¹/₄ teaspoon freshly ground black pepper

³/₄ cup store-bought **GF** or homemade teriyaki sauce (page 26), divided

1 teaspoon grated orange zest (from 1 orange)

12 small bamboo skewers, soaked in water for 15 minutes, or use metal skewers

Thread the chicken, green onion, green pepper, and mushrooms onto the prepared skewers, alternating the chicken and vegetables. Leave a bit of space between each piece to encourage even cooking. Transfer the threaded skewers to a plate. Brush the oil over the chicken and vegetables and then sprinkle with the salt and pepper.

Preheat the grill to medium. Put about ¹/₃ cup of the teriyaki sauce in a small bowl for basting. Mix the orange zest with the remaining teriyaki sauce to use as a dipping sauce. Oil the grill racks to keep the chicken from sticking. Grill the skewers, turning occasionally and basting with the reserved teriyaki sauce, until browned and cooked through, about 12 minutes. Serve with the teriyaki-orange dipping sauce.

VARIATIONS Skewer 1¹/₂ pounds large shrimp, cubes of steak, or chicken breast instead of the chicken thighs. And try zucchini, asparagus, or cherry tomatoes instead of the mushrooms, peppers, or onions. You can also choose just one of the vegetables for the skewers instead of all three.

HEADS UP

If you choose to make your own teriyaki sauce (page 26) for this recipe, you can prepare it up to 2 weeks ahead.

Grilled Pork Satay

SERVES 4 AS A MAIN DISH, 6 AS AN APPETIZER

I enjoy the bold flavors of this marinade on pork or chicken, but you can experiment with shrimp as well. Even though some of the marinade cooks right onto the meat, it's important to give it time to do its job. Mix up the marinade and toss it with the pork in the morning or even the day before and leave the skewering and grilling until right before dinner. Serve the skewers as an appetizer or on top of Vietnamese Rice Noodle Salad (page 84).

1¹/₂ pounds boneless center-cut pork chops

3 cloves garlic, minced

1 medium shallot, minced

1 stalk lemongrass, bottom third only, peeled and finely minced, or grated zest of 1 lemon

1 tablespoon minced fresh ginger

1 tablespoon light brown sugar

1¹/₂ teaspoons ground coriander

1 teaspoon ground cumin

¹/₂ teaspoon turmeric

1 teaspoon Sriracha or other chili-garlic sauce GF

¹/₂ cup well-stirred unsweetened coconut milk

2¹/₂ tablespoons freshly squeezed lime juice (about 2 limes)

2 tablespoons vegetable oil, plus more for oiling the grill

1 tablespoon soy sauce or tamari GF

³/₄ teaspoon salt

12 small bamboo skewers, soaked in water for 15 minutes, or use metal skewers

Peanut Satay Sauce (page 31), for serving

Put the meat in the freezer for 20 minutes to firm it up for slicing. Meanwhile, combine the garlic, shallot, lemongrass, ginger, brown sugar, coriander, cumin, turmeric, and Sriracha in a bowl. Stir to form a paste. Whisk in the coconut milk, lime juice, oil, and soy sauce.

Remove the meat from the freezer and slice it, lengthwise, into 24 thin strips. Put the meat in a glass baking dish or a gallon-size resealable bag and add the marinade. Toss well to coat. Refrigerate for at least 8 hours and up to 24 hours—more time equals more flavor.

Preheat the grill to medium-high. Thread 2 slices of pork onto each of the 12 prepared skewers, leaving a bit of space between each piece to encourage even cooking. Sprinkle the pork with salt. Oil the grill racks. Grill the skewers, turning once, until browned and cooked through, about 3 minutes per side. Serve hot with the peanut sauce.

VARIATION Substitute 1¹/₂ pounds of boneless, skinless chicken breast, large shrimp, salmon cubes, or beef tenderloin for the pork.

....

HEADS UP
Freeze the meat for 20 minutes for easier slicing.
You'll need to marinate the meat for at least 8 hours and up to 24 hours. The dish calls for Peanut Satay Sauce (page 31). You can prepare it up to 1 week ahead.

Halibut Satay *with Thai Cucumber Relish*

SERVES 4 AS A MAIN DISH, 6 AS AN APPETIZER

Grilling fish requires a few preliminary precautions to keep it from sticking, but the result is well worth the preparation necessary. After coating the fish with a bit of oil, put it directly onto a well-oiled, hot grill grate—a cold grate will definitely promote sticking. To oil the grate, put a few tablespoons of oil on a wadded-up paper towel and, using tongs, run the paper towel over the grate. Another trick is to place a separate nonstick or stainless steel grill grid (mine looks like a screen) directly on top of the grill grates to keep smaller pieces from slipping through.

½ cup well-stirred unsweetened coconut milk

4 teaspoons red curry paste **GF**, such as Thai Kitchen

2 teaspoons brown sugar

2 teaspoons Asian fish sauce

1½ pounds halibut fillet, about 1 inch thick, skinned and cut into 1-inch cubes

1 tablespoon vegetable oil, plus more for oiling the grill

¾ teaspoon salt

Lime wedges, for serving

Thai Cucumber Relish (page 115), for serving

Small bamboo skewers, soaked in water for 15 minutes, or use metal skewers

In a large bowl, whisk together the coconut milk, curry paste, brown sugar, and fish sauce. Add the halibut and toss to combine. Let the fish marinate in the refrigerator for about 1 hour.

Preheat the grill to medium-high. Remove the fish from the bowl and wipe off any excess marinade. (This will encourage the fish to brown. If there's too much liquid it will steam.) Thread the halibut onto the prepared skewers, leaving a bit of space between each piece to encourage even cooking. Rub the oil over the fish with your fingers and then sprinkle with salt. Oil the grill racks. Grill the fish, turning once, until browned and cooked through, about 3 minutes per side. Alternatively, cook the halibut under a broiler, about 4 inches from the heat, for approximately 5 minutes. Serve the skewers with a squeeze of lime and the cucumber relish.

VARIATIONS If halibut isn't available, try another firm, meaty seafood such as salmon, shrimp, or sea scallops.

Peanut Satay Sauce (page 31) would also taste great with the satay. Use it instead of or in addition to the cucumbers.

HEADS UP
You'll need to marinate the fish for about 1 hour. The dish calls for Thai Cucumber Relish (page 115). You can prepare it up to 1 day ahead.

Lemongrass Shrimp Skewers

 SERVES 4 AS A MAIN DISH, 6 AS AN APPETIZER

Fancier Vietnamese restaurants often serve sugar cane shrimp, which is seasoned shrimp paste wrapped around a sugar cane stalk. Sugar cane is quite hard to find. As an alternative, I wrap the shrimp around the fat end of a halved lemongrass stalk. This fun presentation is perfect for entertaining, but you can also form the shrimp paste into mini burgers for an easy family meal. If you do come across sugar cane, either fresh or canned, give that a try. In addition to being a tasty appetizer, the shrimp skewers are also delicious with Vietnamese Rice Noodle Salad (page 84).

1 pound raw shrimp, peeled and deveined

6 cloves garlic, smashed

3 green onions, white and green parts, cut into 1-inch lengths

2 teaspoons brown sugar

1 teaspoon Asian fish sauce

Grated zest of 1 lemon or lime

1/2 teaspoon salt

1/4 teaspoon freshly ground black pepper

1 tablespoon vegetable oil, plus more for greasing hands and grill

1 teaspoon cornstarch

3/4 teaspoon baking powder

4 fat stalks lemongrass, bottom 5 inches only, halved lengthwise to form 8 "skewers"

Nuoc cham (page 27), for serving

HEADS UP

You'll need to freeze the shrimp mixture for about 20 minutes. The dish calls for *nuoc cham* (page 27). You can prepare it up to 2 weeks ahead.

In a bowl, toss the shrimp with the garlic, green onions, brown sugar, fish sauce, lemon zest, salt, pepper, and oil. Put the shrimp mixture in the freezer to chill for 20 minutes.

Transfer the shrimp mixture to a food processor and pulse until the shrimp are coarsely chopped, about ten (1-second) pulses. Scrape down the bowl with a rubber spatula. Add the cornstarch and baking powder and pulse two or three more times to combine. The shrimp should be finely chopped with all the ingredients well incorporated into a coarse paste; you should not have a completely smooth paste. If you do not have a food processor, chop the ingredients very finely with a knife. Do not use a blender or you will end up with an inconsistent, gooey mess.

With oiled hands, form about 3 tablespoons of the shrimp paste into a 3-inch-long oval. Gently press a lemongrass stick halfway into the oval. Use your hands to form the shrimp mixture around the lemongrass. It should look like a sausage on a stick. Repeat with the remaining lemongrass and shrimp to form 8 skewers. Alternatively, form the shrimp into eight 2 1/2-inch-diameter patties. Refrigerate, covered, until ready to cook, up to several hours.

Preheat the grill to medium. If possible, oil a smaller grate that you set on top of the grill rack; otherwise, just oil the grill racks. If the shrimp mixture is not already coated with oil, use your hands to lightly coat it with oil (you should only need 1 to 2 teaspoons on your hands). Cook the shrimp, turning occasionally, until pink in color and springy, but not firm, to the touch, about 6 minutes total. Alternatively, cook the shrimp in a nonstick frying pan over medium heat for about 3 minutes per side. Serve with the *nuoc cham* sauce and do not eat the lemongrass.

Miso Glazed Scallops

 SERVES 4 AS A MAIN DISH, 6 AS AN APPETIZER

Leave the bay scallops in the bay and find some fat, jumbo sea scallops for this recipe. The inherently sweet, yet briny taste of the scallops is only enhanced by the same qualities in the glaze. Because sea scallops can be very expensive, we often enjoy the marinade on big chunks of skewered hanger steak as well. Or cook some of each for "surf and turf."

2/3 cup Savory Miso Glaze (page 29)

1 1/2 pounds large sea scallops

Small bamboo skewers, soaked in water for 15 minutes, or use metal skewers

Lemon wedges, for serving

HEADS UP
The dish calls for Savory Miso Glaze (page 29). You can prepare it up to 1 week ahead. You'll need to marinate the scallops for at least 8 hours and up to 24 hours.

If you have just made the miso glaze, cool it completely before marinating the scallops. Put the scallops in a gallon-size resealable bag or a glass baking dish and add the miso glaze. Let the scallops marinate, refrigerated, for at least 8 hours and up to 24 hours, turning the bag occasionally to coat the scallops thoroughly. More time equals more flavor.

Preheat the grill to medium-high. Thread the scallops onto the prepared skewers. Leave a bit of space between each scallop to ensure even cooking. Oil the grill racks. Grill the skewers, turning once, until browned and cooked through, about 3 minutes per side. Serve with a squeeze of fresh lemon juice.

VARIATION Cut 1 1/2 pounds hanger steak into approximately 2 by 1-inch pieces. Marinate and cook in the same manner as the scallops.

Roasted Pork Meatballs

 SERVES 4 AS A MAIN DISH, 6 AS AN APPETIZER

Friend and neighbor Torie Laurent of Indulge Catering in Portland created these vibrant nuggets of flavor, erasing any childhood memories of brown gravy-soaked meatballs. Form the meatballs ahead of time and pop them in the oven at the last minute for an easy party appetizer. Or serve them as a main dish over Vietnamese Rice Noodle Salad (page 84).

1½ pounds ground pork

8 green onions, white and green parts, minced

7 cloves garlic, minced

2 stalks lemongrass, bottom 4 inches only, peeled and minced, or substitute the grated zest of 2 lemons

3 tablespoons chopped fresh cilantro

1½ tablespoons sugar

1½ tablespoons Asian fish sauce

¾ teaspoon salt

3 tablespoons cornstarch

Nuoc cham (page 27) or Spicy Mango Sauce (page 32), for serving

Lettuce leaves, hoisin sauce **GF**, Carrot and Daikon Pickle (page 114), and fresh cilantro, for serving (optional)

In a large bowl, combine the pork, green onions, garlic, lemongrass, cilantro, sugar, fish sauce, and salt. Stir to combine the ingredients. Refrigerate, covered, so the flavors have a chance to marry, at least 3 hours and up to 24 hours. More time equals more flavor.

Preheat the oven to 425°F. Oil a baking sheet. Stir the cornstarch into the meat mixture. Form the meat into twenty-four 1½-inch meatballs. (You can form the meatballs several hours ahead of time. Keep them refrigerated until ready to cook.) Transfer the meatballs to the prepared baking sheet. Cook the meatballs until browned and cooked through, turning once with a spatula, 12 to 15 minutes.

For serving, skewer the meatballs with toothpicks and arrange them on a serving platter with the *nuoc cham* or mango sauce for dipping. Alternatively, using lettuce leaves as wrappers, spread a bit of hoisin sauce on each lettuce leaf and add a meatball, some of the pickle, and a few cilantro leaves.

VARIATION For a juicy, coarse-textured meatball, substitute pork loin, cut into 1-inch cubes, for the ground pork. Toss the cubes with the ingredients in the first step and then freeze the mixture for 20 minutes. Transfer the mixture to a food processor and pulse until the pork is coarsely chopped, about twenty (1-second) pulses. Proceed with the recipe, including the marinating time.

HEADS UP

You'll need to marinate the pork for at least 3 hours and up to 24 hours. The dish calls for *nuoc cham* (page 27) or Spicy Mango Sauce (page 32). You can prepare the *nuoc cham* up to 2 weeks ahead, or the mango sauce up to 3 days ahead.

Porcupine Balls

 SERVES 4 AS AN APPETIZER

I like to call these rice-studded pork meatballs "porcupine balls" because the rice coating makes them look a little like porcupines, plus it amuses my kids more than their other name, "pearly rice balls." No worries if you don't have a bamboo steamer; you can use a metal steamer insert that fits in a regular pot, or see page 21 for more instructions on fashioning your own steamer. Note that you will probably need to steam the meatballs in batches.

1 cup medium-grain rice, soaked in water for at least 4 hours

1 pound ground pork

1/3 cup chopped water chestnuts (canned is fine)

6 green onions, white and green parts, chopped

1 1/2 tablespoons grated fresh ginger

2 teaspoons soy sauce or tamari GF

1 teaspoon toasted sesame oil

1 egg, beaten

1 teaspoon salt

1/2 teaspoon freshly ground black pepper

Soy Vinegar Dipping Sauce (page 26), for serving

HEADS UP

You'll need to soak the rice for at least 4 hours and up to 12 hours. The dish calls for Soy Vinegar Dipping Sauce (page 26). You can prepare it up to 1 week ahead.

Soak the rice in a bowl of water for at least 4 hours and up to 12 hours. Drain the rice well in a colander and then spread it on a baking sheet.

In a bowl, combine the pork, water chestnuts, green onions, ginger, soy sauce, sesame oil, egg, salt, and pepper. Mix the ingredients until well combined. With wet hands, form the mixture into 24 meatballs. (If the meat mixture is too soft to form, put it in the refrigerator for about 15 minutes to firm up.) Gently roll each meatball in the rice. Do not smash the rice into the meat; you want a round, rice-coated meatball. Transfer the meatballs to a plate and refrigerate, covered, until ready to cook. The meatballs can be made several hours ahead. (*Note:* At this point, you can freeze the meatballs and steam them later from frozen. Freeze the formed meatballs on a plate or tray, then transfer to a freezer bag. Add 5 minutes to the cooking time.)

Bring several inches of water to a boil in a wok or large pot. Oil the tray of a bamboo or metal steamer (or line it with parchment paper) and add the meatballs. Steam the meatballs over the boiling water, covered, until the meat and rice are cooked, about 20 minutes per batch. Serve the meatballs hot with the dipping sauce.

VARIATION You can make the meatballs with medium-grain rice, long-grain rice, or even sticky rice. The results are slightly different, yet all work.

Korean-Style Chicken Tacos

 SERVES 4 AS A MAIN DISH, 6 AS AN APPETIZER

If you live on the West Coast, you've probably noticed the explosion of Korean taco trucks, one Asian fusion trend I'm happy to enjoy. Sweet or spicy Korean meats wrapped in warm corn tortillas, topped with a touch of something crisp makes a brilliant combination and darned fine snack! Look for very small (5-inch-diameter) corn tortillas; larger ones will mask the flavor of the chicken. Don't skip the lime wedges for serving; a little squeeze of lime juice adds acidity and mixes with the kimchi to form a sauce.

4 cloves garlic, minced

1¹/₂ teaspoons minced fresh ginger

3 tablespoons mirin

3 tablespoons Korean chili powder, or substitute 2¹/₂ tablespoons paprika mixed with ¹/₄ teaspoon cayenne pepper

2¹/₂ tablespoons sugar

2 tablespoons soy sauce or tamari **GF**

2 teaspoons toasted sesame oil

¹/₂ teaspoon freshly ground black pepper

1¹/₂ pounds boneless, skinless chicken thighs

Small corn tortillas (about 5 inches diameter), for serving

¹/₂ English cucumber, cut into matchsticks

1 cup bean sprouts

¹/₂ cup chopped kimchi **GF**

Lime wedges, for serving

In a small bowl, whisk together the garlic, ginger, mirin, chili powder, sugar, soy sauce, sesame oil, and black pepper. Put the chicken in a glass baking dish or a gallon-size resealable bag and add the marinade. Marinate the chicken for up to 1 hour at room temperature, or refrigerate for up to 24 hours. More time equals more flavor.

Preheat the grill to medium. (Keep the heat medium or the sugar in the marinade will burn.) Oil the grill racks. Remove the chicken from the marinade, wiping off any excess. Grill the chicken until cooked through, about 8 minutes per side. Remove the chicken from the grill and cut it into bite-size pieces.

Wrap the tortillas in a damp paper towel and microwave until hot, about 40 seconds. Alternatively, wrap them in aluminum foil and heat them in a 350°F oven. Spoon about ¹/₄ cup of the chicken onto each tortilla. Top the chicken with some cucumber strips, bean sprouts, and kimchi. Squeeze a little lime juice over the top. Serve immediately.

VARIATION Use *bulgogi* (page 165) in place of the chicken. Or try chicken breasts instead of thighs and grill for about 6 minutes per side.

Instead of corn tortillas, wrap the filling in Mandarin Pancakes (page 68). Or use rice paper, following the instructions for wrapping Salad Rolls with Crab and Spicy Mango Sauce (page 51). Squeeze the lime juice over the filling before wrapping.

HEADS UP
You'll need to marinate the chicken for at least 1 hour and up to 24 hours.

Salad Rolls *with Crab and Spicy Mango Sauce*

 SERVES 6 TO 8 AS AN APPETIZER

Don't let working with rice paper intimidate you; I promise it will be old hat after you finish the first few rolls. Besides, you'll want to master the technique as part of your gluten-free arsenal. Once you learn the process, you can craft salad rolls using any ingredients you like, even ones that aren't Asian!

3 ounces dried rice vermicelli

3/4 pound cooked, picked crabmeat (do not use imitation crab; it often contains gluten)

2 carrots, peeled and shredded

1 small red bell pepper, cut into very thin slices

1 cup shredded lettuce, such as butter or Boston

1/2 cup shredded daikon radish

1/2 cup loosely packed fresh cilantro leaves

1/2 cup loosely packed fresh mint leaves

Freshly squeezed juice of 1/2 lime

2 tablespoons Asian fish sauce

16 (8- to 9-inch-diameter) rice paper wrappers (also called spring roll wrappers or spring roll skins), made from rice flour or tapioca flour

Spicy mango sauce (page 32) or peanut satay sauce (page 31), for serving

---

HEADS UP
The dish calls for Spicy Mango Sauce (pag 32). You can prepare it up to 3 days ahead.

Bring a pot of water to a boil. Add the rice noodles. Remove the pan from the heat and let the noodles stand in the water until tender, 5 to 10 minutes depending on the thickness. Drain the noodles in a colander and then rinse with cold water. Squeeze any excess water from the noodles. Cut them into shorter lengths with scissors and then transfer them to a large bowl.

Add the crab, carrots, bell pepper, lettuce, radish, cilantro, and mint to the noodles and toss until well combined. Add the lime juice and fish sauce and toss once more.

Fill a large bowl with warm water. Put 2 of the rice paper wrappers in the water and soak until pliable, about 30 seconds. Carefully remove the wrappers from the water and set them on a clean kitchen towel. Spoon about 1/2 cup of the filling onto the lower third of each rice paper wrapper and arrange the filling, crosswise, into a log, leaving about a 1-inch border. Bring the lower part of the wrapper up over the filling to enclose it. Fold in the sides of the wrapper over the filling, and then roll into a tight cylinder. Press lightly to seal the edges. Transfer the finished rolls to a platter and cover with a damp paper towel. Repeat with the remaining wrappers and filling. The rolls can be assembled several hours ahead. Cover them with a damp paper towel, then plastic wrap, and refrigerate. Serve with the mango sauce or peanut sauce.

VARIATIONS Instead of crab, use cooked chicken (I even use store-bought rotisserie chicken sometimes, assuming it's gluten free), *bulgogi* (page 165), shrimp, tofu, or grilled pork. You will need about 2 cups of bite-size pieces of any of these.

(continued)

(continued from page 51)

As long as the vegetables and herbs equal 3 to 4 cups, you can mix and match them. Try cucumber, bean sprouts, steamed snow peas, or shredded cabbage. Or add chopped green onion, fresh chiles, Thai basil, or chopped peanuts.

Use the rice paper wrappers to make a "sandwich" with roasted chicken, lettuce, and sliced tomato.

LEFT TO RIGHT: Lift the lower part of the wrapper up over the filling to enclose it. Fold the sides of the wrapper over the filling. Roll into a tight cylinder.

Crispy Spring Rolls

 SERVES 6 AS AN APPETIZER

For a few years, I completely wrote off crispy egg roll treats for dead, thinking their wrappers were universally made from wheat flour. While this is often the case with egg rolls, I realized Vietnamese spring rolls use rice paper wrappers instead. You probably don't have a deep fryer, but it's easy to fry these rolls in a regular saucepan or a wok. Grab a candy thermometer from a cookware store to make the process more dependable. And if you feel especially ambitious, make a few extra rolls as a topping for Vietnamese Rice Noodle Salad (page 84). When you're done, strain the cooled oil back into the container and you can reuse it once or twice. If you do order spring rolls in a restaurant, be sure to confirm not only that the ingredients are gluten free, but also that the cooking oil is designated for gluten-free frying only.

½ pound ground pork

½ pound peeled raw shrimp, coarsely chopped

4 shiitake mushrooms, stems removed, caps finely chopped

4 green onions, white and green parts, thinly sliced

2 cloves garlic, minced

1 carrot, peeled and grated

1 tablespoon Asian fish sauce

½ teaspoon salt

¼ teaspoon freshly ground black pepper

1 egg, beaten

12 (8- to 9-inch-diameter) rice paper wrappers (also called spring roll wrappers or spring roll skins), made from rice flour or tapioca flour

Vegetable oil, for frying

Soft lettuce leaves, such as butter lettuce, for serving

Fresh cilantro and/or mint leaves, for serving

Nuoc cham (page 27) or Fiery Ginger Sauce (page 30), for serving

---

HEADS UP

This dish calls for *nuoc cham* or Fiery Ginger Sauce. You can prepare the *nuoc cham* up to 2 weeks ahead, or the ginger sauce up to 3 days ahead.

To make the filling, combine the raw pork, raw shrimp, mushrooms, green onions, garlic, carrot, fish sauce, salt, pepper, and egg in a bowl. Mix well.

Fill a large bowl with warm water. Soak 2 of the rice paper wrappers in the water and let stand until pliable, about 30 seconds. Carefully remove the wrappers from the water and set them on a clean kitchen towel. Spoon about ¼ cup of the filling onto the lower third of each wrapper and arrange the filling, crosswise, into a 5-inch log. Bring the lower part of the wrapper up over the filling to enclose it. Fold in the sides of the wrapper over the filling, and then roll into a tight cylinder. Press lightly to seal the edges. Transfer the finished rolls to a plate. Cover each layer with plastic wrap; the rolls will stick to each other if you stack them. The rolls can be assembled several hours before frying. Cover them with plastic wrap and refrigerate.

In a large saucepan or a wok, heat about 3 inches of oil to 375°F. This may take about 15 minutes over medium heat. (If you don't have a deep-fry thermometer, sprinkle a drop of water in the oil. When it sizzles vigorously, the oil is ready. The oil should not get hot enough to smoke.) Line a plate with paper towels. Carefully add as many of the spring rolls to the pan as will fit without crowding. Fry the rolls, turning occasionally to keep them from sticking together, until crisp and brown, about 8 minutes per batch. Remove the rolls with a slotted spoon and transfer them to the prepared plate. Repeat the process until all the rolls are cooked; be sure to heat the oil back to 375°F between batches.

For serving, cut each spring roll in half. Arrange a halved spring roll on a lettuce leaf and top with a few fresh herbs and a drizzle of sauce. Enclose the roll in the lettuce and enjoy. Or, serve the spring rolls whole with one of the dipping sauces. The spring rolls can be made ahead and reheated in a 350°F oven for about 15 minutes.

VARIATION It can be hard to find 6-inch-diameter rice paper, but if you can get your hands on some I really prefer making 16 smaller spring rolls. Use 2 tablespoons of filling per roll.

FOUR Dumplings and Savory Pancakes

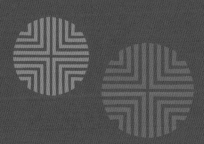

As a working mother of two children, I am sensitive to busy schedules and time constraints. I have a battery of recipes I work from during the week and others I save for weekends. This chapter is filled with weekend recipes. When it comes down to it, if you want a dumpling or pancake that's gluten free, you probably need to make it yourself. These recipes inherently take time because they contain multiple steps: making the wrappers and fillings; forming and cooking the dumplings; crafting a sauce. Whenever possible, I list make-ahead, reheating, or even freezing instructions. You should set aside a chunk of time on your first run-through, but ultimately your timing will improve with familiarity. None of the recipes are difficult, merely a little time-consuming.

Converting traditional wheat-based dumpling wrappers into gluten-free versions takes some fancy footwork (like the pot stickers in this chapter), but I also discovered a whole world of fabulous dumplings that are naturally gluten free. Many Asian dumplings enlist white rice flour, sweet rice flour, tapioca, cornstarch, chickpea flour, or actual grains of rice as the base of their dough. The resulting dumplings differ from their wheat-based cousins, mostly in texture, but are delicious in their own right. In addition to the pot stickers, I introduce one dumpling based on sweet rice flour and a uniquely textured tapioca dumpling. Because they can be time-consuming, I offer only an introduction to gluten-free dumplings so as not to take space away from other recipes that you might prepare on a more regular basis. If you find yourself intrigued, check the library for old-school Chinese, Thai, and Vietnamese cookbooks; they may reveal recipes for many of these naturally gluten-free treats.

One comment about ordering dumplings in a restaurant: If you live near a very traditional Asian restaurant, they may serve some of these less common, naturally gluten-free dumplings. I urge you to double-check with the kitchen that they are truly gluten free. I spoke with a few restaurant chefs who told me while they do offer sweet rice flour or tapioca dumplings, sometimes they add "just a little" wheat flour to make the dough easier to work. Yes, that would make things easier, wouldn't it?

Sticky Rice Dumplings *with Chicken and Mushrooms*

 MAKES 16 DUMPLINGS

After reading Andrea Nguyen's fantastic book, Asian Dumplings, *I was inspired to create my own version of banh it, stuffed round dumplings made from sweet rice flour. My dumplings house a non-traditional filling of ground chicken and chopped shiitake mushrooms inside a soft, chewy dough vaguely reminiscent of a steamed bun. The flour, ground from grains of sticky rice, is commonly known as glutinous flour (glutinous refers to its sticky texture, not the presence of gluten) or sweet rice flour. I made several batches using different brands of sweet rice flour and my favorite was Koda Farms Mochiko Blue Star sweet rice flour. I found the other brands needed a touch less water in the dough and a bit more oil on the hands for shaping the dumplings. If you use a different brand, start out easy on the water and work the dough to a Play-Doh-like consistency. (Incidentally, Play-Doh is not gluten free; do not eat it.)*

---

1 tablespoon vegetable oil, plus more for oiling hands

¹⁄₄ cup finely chopped onion

¹⁄₄ pound shiitake mushrooms, stems removed, caps finely chopped

¹⁄₂ pound ground chicken, preferably dark meat

³⁄₄ teaspoon salt, divided

¹⁄₄ teaspoon freshly ground black pepper

1 tablespoon soy sauce or tamari GF, plus more for serving

2 cups sweet rice flour, plus more for dusting the counter

1 cup cold water

Nuoc cham (page 27), for serving (optional)

First make the filling. In a frying pan, heat the oil over medium heat. Add the onion and cook, stirring occasionally, until it starts to soften, about 2 minutes. Raise the heat to medium-high and add the mushrooms. Cook until the mushrooms shrink and start to brown, about 3 minutes. Stir in the chicken, ¹⁄₄ teaspoon of the salt, and the pepper and cook, breaking the chicken into very small pieces (large pieces will tear the dough) with a wooden spoon or spatula, until it loses its raw color, about 3 minutes longer. Stir in the soy sauce. Transfer the filling to a bowl and set aside to cool. (The filling will keep, covered, in the refrigerator for up to 2 days.)

In a bowl, combine the sweet rice flour and the remaining ¹⁄₂ teaspoon of salt. Using a fork, stir in all but 2 tablespoons of the cold water and mix well until a rough dough starts to form. Add the remaining water if needed. Dust your hands and the counter with sweet rice flour. Transfer the dough to the counter and knead it until smooth. The dough should not be sticky; if it is, work in a bit of extra flour, about 1 tablespoon at a time, and up to 3 tablespoons. Divide the dough in half and roll each half into a 12-inch-long rope. Cut each rope into 8 equal pieces, for a total of 16 pieces of dough. Roll each piece into a ping-pong-size ball. Put the dough back in the bowl and cover it with a clean kitchen towel or plastic wrap so it does not dry out.

To form the dumplings, lightly oil a dinner plate. With lightly oiled hands, flatten a piece of dough into a circle with the heel of your hand. Pick it up and rotate the dough in your hand, pressing it with your fingers, to form a 3-inch circle. Hold the dough in one hand and spoon 1 tablespoon of filling into the center of the circle. Lift the sides of the dough (curling your fingers will help lift one side), forming a half-moon shape around the filling, and seal the edges by pressing them together with your fingers. Very gently form the dumpling into a golf-ball-size round. Repair any tiny holes by pressing the dough back together with your fingers. Transfer the finished dumpling to the prepared plate and cover loosely with plastic wrap. Repeat with the remaining dough and filling, forming 16 dumplings. At this point you can refrigerate the dumplings, covered, until you're ready to cook them, up to 8 hours ahead.

Bring several inches of water to a boil in a large pot or a wok. Oil the tray of a bamboo or metal steamer (or line it with parchment paper) and add the dumplings to the steamer, leaving a little space between each dumpling for them to expand. (You can also set a small, oiled plate on a rack in your wok; if you don't have a steamer see page 21 for details on crafting your own.) Steam the dumplings, covered, over the boiling water, in batches if necessary, for 15 minutes. Check the pan occasionally to make sure there's enough water; add more if needed. Remove the dumplings from the steamer and let them stand for about 10 minutes to firm up. Serve the dumplings hot with *nuoc cham* or soy sauce. Refrigerate any leftovers, covered and in one layer, for up to 2 days. Reheat the dumplings in the microwave or re-steam them for 10 minutes.

VARIATION Instead of the chicken and mushroom filling, use half the amount of filling from steamed Rice Sheets with Pork and Shrimp Filling (page 76), or double the filling from Tapioca Dumplings with Beef and Shallots (page 62).

Gingery Pork Pot Stickers

 MAKES 28 DUMPLINGS

Many types of Asian dumpling wrappers are actually based on naturally gluten-free flours, such as rice or tapioca, but the beloved pot sticker remains a wheat dough through and through. Creating a great alternative took some tinkering, but I think you will be very pleased with the results. The recipe calls for "just boiled" water. After you turn off the heat, let the water cool for about 30 seconds to let the bubbles recede before measuring. It makes the process much safer. I like pot stickers best hot out of the pan, but you can freeze some before cooking if you don't plan to finish them all in one meal. They cook well right from the freezer.

---

¹/₂ cup tapioca flour (also called tapioca starch)

¹/₂ cup millet flour

¹/₂ cup sweet rice flour, plus plenty more for rolling out the dough

1¹/₂ teaspoons xanthan gum

³/₄ teaspoon salt, divided

¹/₂ cup boiling water

2 tablespoons cold water

³/₄ pound ground pork

3 green onions, white and green parts, minced

1 tablespoon minced fresh ginger

2 teaspoons soy sauce or tamari GF

¹/₂ teaspoon toasted sesame oil

¹/₄ teaspoon freshly ground black pepper

3 tablespoons vegetable oil, divided

Soy Vinegar Dipping Sauce (page 26), for serving

To make the dough, stir together the tapioca flour, millet flour, sweet rice flour, xanthan gum, and ¹/₂ teaspoon salt in a bowl. Add the just-boiled water and stir with a fork to combine. Add the cold water and mix well until a dough starts to form. Use your hands to knead the dough together a few times—you can do this right in the bowl—and then form the dough into two balls. Transfer the dough to a large resealable bag until ready to use, up to several hours.

In a second bowl, combine the raw pork, green onions, ginger, soy sauce, sesame oil, remaining ¹/₄ teaspoon salt, and pepper. Mix well to combine.

To form the dumplings, dust your hands, the counter, and a baking sheet with sweet rice flour. Roll one piece of the dough into a long rope, about ³/₄ inch thick. Cut the dough into 14 pieces and put them back into the resealable bag. Repeat with the other ball of dough for a total of 28 pieces. The dough will dry out quickly; make sure it stays covered.

Keep plenty of sweet rice flour nearby (up to ¹/₂ cup) for dusting the counter and the rolling pin to prevent the dough from sticking. Working with one piece of dough at a time, flatten the dough into a circle with the heel of your hand. Using a small rolling pin—a small dowel works best—roll the dough into a 3- to 3¹/₂-inch circle, turning the dough periodically

(continued)

(continued from page 58)

HEADS UP

The dish calls for Soy Vinegar
Dipping Sauce. You can prepare it up to 1 week ahead.

to prevent sticking. (Alternately, put the dough between two
pieces of plastic wrap and roll it into a circle.) Transfer the
dumpling wrappers to the prepared baking sheet. Repeat with
the remaining dough. (If you run out of space on the baking
sheet, make a second layer separated by plastic wrap.)

Dust a dinner plate with sweet rice flour. Spoon a scant
tablespoon of filling into the center of each wrapper. Dip
two fingers in a small bowl of water and run them around
half the circumference of each circle. (This is so the wet side
can stick to the dry side.) Lift the sides, forming a half-moon
shape around the filling; keep the bottom flat against your
hand or the counter. Pinch the dough together at the top and
then form two or three pleats along each side; press to seal.
(Alternatively, if you have a dumpling press, use it to form and
seal the dumplings.) Transfer the dumplings to the prepared
plate. Cover tightly with plastic wrap and refrigerate until
ready to cook, up to 4 hours ahead.

In a large nonstick frying pan, heat 1¹/₂ tablespoons of
the oil over medium-high heat. Add half the dumplings to the
pan and cook until browned on the bottom, 2 to 3 minutes.
Holding the pan lid in one hand (to control splattering), add
¹/₃ cup water to the pan and immediately cover it. Lower the
heat to low and steam the dumplings until cooked through,
8 to 10 minutes. Remove the lid and raise the heat to medium.
Cook until the water evaporates and the bottoms of the dumplings are well browned, about 2 minutes longer. Repeat with
the remaining dumplings and oil. Serve hot with the dipping
sauce or a bowl of soy sauce GF.

Note: If you do not plan on eating the dumplings all at
once (reheating them is fine, not great), freeze some of the
uncooked dumplings for later. Freeze the dumplings on a plate
or tray before transferring them to a freezer bag to keep them
from sticking together. Add the dumplings to the pan straight
from the freezer and increase the steaming time by 2 minutes.

Tapioca Dumplings *with Beef and Shallots*

 MAKES 16 DUMPLINGS

I spent an afternoon with Lucy Eklund and her daughter April, co-owners of Jade: Bistro, Teahouse, & Patisserie, learning the intricacies of tapioca dumplings, or banh bot loc. It fascinated me how just-boiled water (cool it for about 30 seconds before measuring) transformed the tapioca into a smooth, workable dough. For those who grew up eating wheat flour–based dumplings, the texture of tapioca dumplings may come as a bit of a surprise. Their unique, slippery consistency could be somewhat challenging to Western palates, but I think it's worth a try, especially if you're a dumpling lover. Try them with pork and shrimp filling (see Variations) as another, more traditional option.

4 tablespoons vegetable oil, divided

1 large shallot, thinly sliced

1/4 pound ground beef

1/4 teaspoon salt

1/4 teaspoon freshly ground black pepper

1 cup tapioca flour (also called tapioca starch), plus more for dusting

Scant 1/2 cup just-boiled water

4 green onions, white and green parts, thinly sliced

Nuoc cham (page 27), for serving

HEADS UP

The dish calls for *nuoc cham* (page 27). You can prepare it up to 2 weeks ahead.

To make the filling, heat 1 tablespoon of the oil in a large, nonstick frying pan, over medium-high heat. Add the shallot and cook, stirring occasionally, until it starts to brown, about 3 minutes. Add the ground beef and cook, breaking it into very small pieces (large pieces will tear the dough) with a wooden spoon or spatula, until no longer pink, about 5 minutes. Transfer the filling to a small bowl and season with the salt and pepper. (The filling will keep, covered, in the refrigerator for up to 2 days.) Wipe out the pan and set it aside for finishing the dumplings.

Combine the tapioca flour and a pinch of salt in a bowl. Pour the just-boiled water and 1 tablespoon of the oil over the tapioca and stir with a fork. Keep stirring until it forms a dough; it should come together after a minute or so, but if it needs more water, add about 1 tablespoon. Do not add more water than that; the dough should not be sticky. Dust your hands and the counter with some tapioca flour. Knead the dough until smooth, about 2 minutes, and then roll the dough into a 3/4-inch-thick rope. Cut the dough into 16 pieces and transfer them to a gallon-size resealable bag. The dough will dry out quickly; make sure it stays covered. Keep the dough at room temperature until ready to use, up to 4 hours.

Lightly oil a dinner plate. To form the dumplings, working with one piece of dough at a time, flatten the dough into a circle with the heel of your hand. Pick it up (with lightly tapioca-floured hands if necessary) and rotate the dough in your hand, pressing it between your fingers and thumbs, to form a 2^1/$_2$-inch round. Spoon 1 teaspoon of filling into the center of the dough round. Lift the sides, forming a half-moon shape around the filling, and seal the edges by pressing them together with your fingers. Transfer the finished dumpling to the prepared plate. Repeat with the remaining dough and filling, forming 16 dumplings. You can refrigerate the formed dumplings, covered with plastic wrap, until ready to cook, up to 6 hours.

Bring a large saucepan of water to a boil. Add a splash of vegetable oil and half the dumplings to the pan; simmer gently until the dumplings float to the surface, about 2 minutes. Turn the dumplings with a spoon and cook until nearly translucent, 2 to 3 minutes longer. Remove the dumplings with a slotted spoon and transfer them to a bowl of cold water to remove excess starch; the dumplings are very sticky. Repeat with the remaining dumplings.

For serving, heat 1 tablespoon of the oil in the nonstick frying pan over medium-high heat. Add half the green onions and cook until sizzling and wilted, about 1 minute; lower the heat to medium-low. Remove half the dumplings from the water with a slotted spoon (let as much water as possible drain off) and add them to the pan. Do not crowd the dumplings or they may stick together. Turn the dumplings to coat with the green onions and oil and then transfer them to a serving plate. Repeat with the remaining 1 tablespoon oil, green onions, and dumplings. Serve with *nuoc cham*. Use a microwave to reheat the dumplings.

VARIATION Substitute ground pork for the ground beef, or use about one-third of the filling from Steamed Rice Sheets with Pork and Shrimp Filling (page 76).

Steamed Radish Cake

MAKES 50 (1-INCH) CUBES

My friend Sarah introduced me to the notion of radish cake, a favorite from her time living in Singapore. Chinese versions (often called "turnip cake") combine grated radishes or turnips with flavorful ingredients (dried shrimp, mushrooms, Chinese sausage) suspended in a rice flour batter and steamed; it is often cubed and served as dim sum. The Singaporean version (locally known as "carrot cake") is more austere and I followed suit, keeping the recipe basic, but I also included a separate recipe for incorporating the radish cake into a stir-fry. Try part of this cake simply sautéed in vegetable oil or—my preference—bacon fat for an unusual breakfast (I cook a few pieces at a time throughout the week) and save the other half for Singapore Carrot Cake (page 67). I strongly prefer using a Thai brand of rice flour, such as Erawan, for the radish cake. Other brands will work, but will produce a slightly gummy cake.

---

2 pounds daikon radish, peeled

1¼ teaspoons salt, divided

1½ cups white rice flour (I use Erawan brand)

1 teaspoon sugar

Vegetable oil or bacon fat, for cooking

Soy sauce or tamari **GF**, for serving

....

HEADS UP
The radish cake needs to chill for at least 4 hours or overnight.

Grate the radish on the large holes of a box grater or with the grating attachment of a food processor. Measure 4 cups of grated radish—do not use more—and add it to a saucepan with 1 teaspoon of the salt and 2 tablespoons of water. Cover the pan and turn the heat to medium. When the water starts steaming, lower the heat to medium-low and cook, covered, stirring occasionally, until the radish is translucent, about 25 minutes.

Generously oil a 9-inch round cake pan. In a mixing bowl, stir together the rice flour, the remaining ¼ teaspoon salt, and the sugar. Strain the radish in a sieve set over a large measuring cup to collect the liquid. Press down on the radish with a large spoon to remove most of the liquid. Add enough water to the measuring cup to equal 1 cup. Let the liquid cool to lukewarm. Stir the liquid into the rice flour until smooth, and then add the radish. Stir to combine. The batter should look similar to tapioca pudding. (If the liquid is too hot, it will start to cook the rice flour, forming more of a dough. If this happens, it's okay; just spread the batter evenly in the pan with your hands or a wooden spoon.) Transfer the batter to the prepared pan. Put the cake pan in a steamer set over a pot of boiling water and steam, covered, over medium-high heat for 1 hour. (You can also set a small, oiled plate on a rack in your wok; if you don't have a steamer see page 21 for details on crafting your own.) Check the pan occasionally to make sure the water does not run dry; add more if needed. Remove the cake pan from the steamer with tongs and let cool to room temperature.

Run a knife around the edge of the radish cake and invert the pan onto a plate to remove the cake. (If the radish cake sticks, cut out a small piece, and then remove the rest with a spatula. You will eventually cut it into pieces anyway.) Refrigerate the radish cake, covered with plastic wrap, for at least 4 hours or overnight. The radish cake will keep, covered, in the refrigerator for up to 1 week.

For serving, cut the radish cake into 1-inch cubes. Pat the cubes dry with a paper towel or clean kitchen towel to remove any moisture. In a large nonstick frying pan, heat about 1 tablespoon of oil or bacon fat over medium-high heat. Add half the radish cake cubes and cook, turning occasionally, until well browned, 6 to 8 minutes. Repeat with the remaining radish cake or save the rest for later. Serve hot with soy sauce for dipping.

Singapore Carrot Cake

 SERVES 4 AS A SIDE DISH

Imagine my surprise when I first ordered "carrot cake" in a Southeast Asian restaurant and received a savory dish of marvelously crusted cubes of radish "cake" stir-fried with eggs, vegetables, and a lightly sweetened sauce. The "cake" part consists of steamed radishes suspended in a batter of rice flour and water. I haven't figured out the "carrot" part, but I found the whole combination so bizarre and delicious that I had to come up with a version myself. As it stands, my favorite time to eat carrot cake is for breakfast, but you can serve it any time. My husband and I enjoy it as a main dish for two.

3 tablespoons vegetable oil, divided

Half recipe Steamed Radish Cake (page 64), about 25 (1-inch) cubes

1 small onion, thinly sliced

3 cloves garlic, minced

3 green onions, white and green parts, cut into 1-inch lengths

1 large handful bean sprouts

3 eggs, beaten with a pinch of salt

1½ tablespoons kecap manis **GF** (see below)

1 teaspoon soy sauce or tamari **GF**

¼ teaspoon salt

½ cup fresh cilantro leaves

In a large nonstick frying pan, heat 1 tablespoon of the oil over medium-high heat. If the radish cake cubes feel wet, pat them dry with paper towels or a clean kitchen towel. Add the radish cakes to the pan in a single layer, frying in batches if necessary, and cook, turning occasionally, until well browned, 6 to 8 minutes. Transfer the radish cakes to a plate.

Heat the remaining 2 tablespoons oil in the same pan over medium-high heat. Add the onion, garlic, and green onions and cook, stirring occasionally, until starting to wilt, about 1 minute. Add the bean sprouts and cook 1 minute longer. Move the vegetables to the side of the pan and pour the eggs in the center. Let the eggs set for about 30 seconds and then scramble them into the vegetables. Return the browned radish cakes to the pan and add the kecap manis, soy sauce, and salt. Cook, tossing, until everything is heated through, about 1 minute. Stir in the cilantro and serve hot.

HEADS UP

The dish calls for Steamed Radish Cake (page 64); it needs to be prepared ahead and chilled for at least 4 hours or overnight.

KECAP MANIS SUBSTITUTE

It can be difficult finding a gluten-free brand of kecap manis, a thick, sweet Indonesian soy sauce, but you can whip up a reasonable substitute in no time. Simmer equal parts brown sugar and soy sauce **GF** in a pan until the sugar dissolves, about 1 minute. Cool before using. I usually make a small batch using ¼ cup of each and keep the rest in the refrigerator, covered, for up to 2 months.

Mandarin Pancakes

 MAKES 16 (5- TO 6-INCH) PANCAKES

If you miss soft, warm Mandarin pancakes as part of your Chinese food experience, I think you'll find this gluten-free version really hits the mark. The pancakes act like a flour tortilla, a perfect vehicle for Mu Shu Pork (page 170), Korean-Style Chicken Tacos (page 49), or leftover shredded Soy Sauce Chicken (page 158). The pancakes taste great, but they do have a rather homemade appearance with shaggy edges. I don't mind this, but if you prefer perfect circles, roll out the dough to a $^1/_{16}$-inch thickness and use a 5- to 6-inch round cutter to form your pancakes. Measure the water about 30 seconds after boiling to keep things safe. Thanks to Kyra Bussanich at Crave Bake Shop for developing this recipe just for us.

$^1/_2$ cup tapioca flour (also called tapioca starch)

$^1/_2$ cup millet flour

$^1/_2$ cup sweet rice flour, plus more for rolling

$1^1/_2$ teaspoons xanthan gum

$^1/_2$ teaspoon salt

$^1/_2$ cup boiling water

2 tablespoons cold water

2 tablespoons toasted sesame oil, plus more if needed

HEADS UP

You can make the pancakes ahead and refrigerate them in an airtight container for up to 2 days or freeze them for up to 1 month.

In a bowl, stir together the tapioca flour, millet flour, sweet rice flour, xanthan gum, and salt. Add the boiling water and stir with a fork to combine. Add the cold water and mix well until a dough starts to form. Use your hands to knead the dough a few times—you can do this right in the bowl—and then form the dough into 4 balls. Divide each dough ball into four pieces for a total of 16. The dough is easiest to work with while it's still warm, but you can transfer the dough to a large resealable bag until ready to use.

Dust the counter and a rolling pin generously with sweet rice flour. (You may use up to $^1/_2$ cup sweet rice flour; don't skimp or the dough will stick.) Flatten one ball of dough with the heel of your hand and then roll it into a very thin pancake, approximately $^1/_{16}$-inch thick and about 5 inches in diameter. (Alternatively, put the dough between two pieces of plastic wrap and roll it into a pancake.) Transfer the pancake to a plate and, using a pastry brush, brush the top of the pancake with sesame oil, covering the entire surface. Roll out a second pancake and lay it on top of the first. Do not brush with oil. Cover the pancakes with a clean kitchen towel. Repeat the process with the remaining dough, making 8 double pancakes, each separated by a layer of sesame oil. You can stack the pancakes on top of one another.

Lay another clean kitchen towel over a small plate. Heat a nonstick frying pan over medium-high heat. Transfer one double-pancake to the pan and cook until you notice the top pancake forming air bubbles on the surface, about 30 seconds. Flip the pancake and cook until the second side forms air bubbles, about 30 seconds longer. You do not want the pancakes to brown or crisp; if they do not bubble, go ahead and flip them. Remove the pancake from the pan while it is still pliable and transfer it to the towel-lined plate. Separate the two pancakes from each other—if they stick together, you didn't use enough oil—and fold the edges of the towel over the pancakes to keep them warm and moist. Repeat with the remaining pairs of pancakes. Serve the pancakes immediately while they are warm. Or make the pancakes earlier in the day and keep the stack at room temperature, covered with plastic wrap. Just before serving, steam them for 10 minutes or wrap the stack of pancakes in a barely damp paper towel and then plastic wrap and microwave them until hot. Keep the steamed pancakes covered with a towel at the table to keep them warm throughout the meal. Leftover pancakes can be refrigerated in an airtight container for up to 2 days or frozen for 1 month. Defrost them in the refrigerator before reheating.

Korean Green Onion Pancakes

 SERVES 6 AS AN APPETIZER

Back in our East Coast days (and before I was gluten free), we frequented our friend Yun Jae's parents' restaurant. Even though there were only two couples, we were always seated at an enormous table, easily big enough for eight. We sat there for hours and hours as delectable Korean specialties appeared at our table. One of my favorites was the pancakes, crisp and hot from the pan, filled with green onions, seafood, and sometimes kimchi. Although that version contained wheat flour, these pancakes survived the switch to rice flour with ease.

---

1 cup white rice flour

1 teaspoon salt

1/2 teaspoon Korean chili powder, or substitute 1/2 teaspoon paprika mixed with a pinch of cayenne pepper

2 eggs, beaten

3/4 cup cold water

6 green onions, white and green parts, thinly sliced

1/4 cup finely diced red bell pepper

1 or 2 jalapeño chiles, thinly sliced

1 1/2 tablespoons vegetable oil, plus more if needed

Soy Vinegar Dipping Sauce (page 26), for serving

HEADS UP
The dish calls for Soy Vinegar Dipping Sauce. You can pre-pare it up to 1 week ahead.

In a bowl, whisk together the rice flour, salt, chile powder, eggs, and cold water. Fold in the green onions, bell pepper, and jalapeño.

Line a plate with paper towels. In a large nonstick frying pan, heat 1/2 tablespoon of the oil over medium-high heat. Stir the batter. Using a 1-cup measure, scoop out a scant cup of the batter and add it to the pan, forming it into a thin pancake. Cook for 3 minutes and then flip the pancake using a spatula. Lower the heat to medium. Continue cooking until the pan-cake is crisp and brown, 3 to 5 minutes longer. Transfer the pancake to the prepared plate. Repeat the process, stirring well before each pancake. Remember to start each pancake over medium-high heat. Serve the pancakes hot from the pan or keep warm in a low oven while you prepare the rest. Cut the pancakes into wedges and serve with the dipping sauce.

VARIATIONS Chopped clams, baby shrimp, shredded carrots, and chopped kimchi **GF** (squeezed dry of its liquid) all make especially tasty pancakes. You'll need about 1/3 cup per pancake.

Savory Mung Bean Pancakes

SERVES 4 TO 6 AS AN APPETIZER

The beauty of these sturdy pancakes (other than great taste) is their ability to reheat with ease. You can make them early in the day and reheat them later in a pan or a 350°F oven. I've even frozen them with great success. If you own a griddle, you can cook multiple pancakes at the same time. Generally, I make big pancakes and cut them into wedges, but you can also make little ones and serve them as a fancy hors d'oeuvre or a kid-friendly dinner. Look for the split mung beans in the dried bean section of upscale grocery stores or Asian markets. I like the added crunch of the bean sprouts, but you can leave them out for a cleaner appearance or one less step. Please note that several of the ingredients are used in both the pancakes and the dipping sauce; keep an eye on the correct quantities for each.

1 cup dried split mung beans (also called *moong dal*)

1 cup less 1 tablespoon water

1 teaspoon salt

4^1/$_2$ tablespoons soy sauce or tamari **GF**, divided

3 teaspoons toasted sesame oil, divided

^{1}/$_2$ teaspoon freshly ground black pepper, divided

4 cloves garlic, minced, divided

^{1}/$_2$ pound ground pork

1 cup chopped bok choy or Napa cabbage

^{1}/$_2$ cup shredded carrot

^{1}/$_2$ cup chopped onion or sliced green onions

3 tablespoons vegetable oil

2 cups bean sprouts (optional)

Soak the mung beans in a bowl of water for at least 4 hours or overnight. Drain the beans in a colander and rinse with cold water. Drain the beans well and then transfer them to a blender. Puree the beans with the water and salt. The consistency should be like a pancake batter, not too thick but definitely pourable.

To make the dipping sauce, in a small bowl, combine 3 tablespoons of the soy sauce, 1^1/$_2$ teaspoons of the sesame oil, ^{1}/$_4$ teaspoon of the black pepper, and one-quarter of the garlic. Set aside until ready to use. The dipping sauce will keep, covered, in the refrigerator for several days.

To make the pancakes, in a bowl, combine the raw pork, bok choy, carrots, onion, and the remaining 1^1/$_2$ tablespoons soy sauce, 1^1/$_2$ teaspoons sesame oil, ^{1}/$_4$ teaspoon black pepper, and three-quarters of the garlic. Mix until well combined. Pour in the bean puree and stir to form a batter.

Line a dinner plate with a paper towel. In a large nonstick frying pan, heat ^{1}/$_2$ tablespoon of the vegetable oil over medium-high heat. Using a 1-cup measure, scoop 1 cup of the batter into the pan, flattening it into approximately a 7-inch round, about ^{1}/$_2$ inch thick. Sprinkle a handful of the bean sprouts on top of each pancake, pressing them into the

(continued)

(continued from page 71)

surface. Cook for 5 minutes and then flip the pancake using a spatula. Continue cooking, adding a bit more oil to the pan if necessary, until the pancake is golden brown, 3 to 5 minutes longer. Transfer the pancake to the prepared plate. Repeat the process, stirring the batter well before scooping out each pancake. (Alternatively, heat an electric griddle to 375°F and cook multiple pancakes at once.) Serve the pancakes hot from the pan or keep them warm in a low oven while you prepare the rest. Cut the pancakes into wedges and serve with the dipping sauce. Leftover pancakes can be refrigerated, covered, for up to 2 days or frozen for up to 1 month. Reheat the pancakes on a parchment-lined baking sheet in a 350°F oven for about 15 minutes or in a dry nonstick frying pan over medium heat.

VARIATION Substitute ground beef or very thinly sliced steak for the pork.

HEADS UP
The dried beans will need to soak for at least 4 hours or overnight.

Shrimp and Sweet Potato Tempura Pancakes

 SERVES 4 TO 6 AS AN APPETIZER

Traditional tempura involves battering shrimp and vegetables piece by piece before dunking them in the deep fryer. Instead, I combine the ingredients into fritters and cook them in a nonstick pan, significantly decreasing the oil and mess. After testing many combinations of flours and starches, I decided on a mix of rice flour and cornstarch for both lightness and flavor. I like the pancakes hot with a little squeeze of lemon, but you can also make a simple dipping sauce by combining equal parts soy sauce GF *and mirin, or try them with Fiery Ginger Sauce (page 30).*

HEADS UP
You can prepare the ginger sauce up to 3 days ahead.

In a bowl, whisk together the rice flour, 1/4 cup of the cornstarch, and the salt. Add the egg and the sparkling water to the bowl and whisk to form a smooth batter.

Pat the shrimp dry with a paper towel; if they are too wet the pancakes will be mushy. Put the shrimp, sweet potato, and

3/4 cup white rice flour

1/4 cup plus 1 tablespoon cornstarch, divided

1/2 teaspoon salt, plus more for sprinkling

1 egg, beaten

1/2 cup plus 2 tablespoons cold sparkling water or club soda

1/2 pound raw, peeled shrimp, deveined and coarsely chopped

1 cup peeled, shredded sweet potato

1 small onion, finely diced

3 tablespoons vegetable oil, plus more if needed

Lemon wedges, for serving

Soy sauce GF or Fiery Ginger Sauce (page 30), for serving (optional)

onion in another bowl. Add the remaining 1 tablespoon cornstarch and toss to combine. Stir the batter and pour it over the shrimp, sweet potato, and onion.

Set a rack over paper towels. Heat 1 tablespoon of the oil in a large nonstick frying pan over medium-high heat. Scoop heaping 1/4-cup measures of the batter into the pan, flattening them into approximately 4-inch pancakes. (My pan fit 4 pancakes at a time, but if you have a griddle you may be able to cook more.) Cook the pancakes until light golden, about 3 minutes. Flip the pancakes and flatten them with a spatula, making them as thin as possible. Cook until golden, about 3 minutes longer. Transfer the pancakes to the rack. Sprinkle a bit of salt over the pancakes while they are hot. Repeat the process, stirring the batter well before each batch, for a total of 12 pancakes. If the pan gets too hot, lower the heat to medium.

Serve the pancakes hot or at room temperature with a squeeze of lemon juice, soy sauce GF, or ginger sauce. After cooling completely, the tempura pancakes can be refrigerated, covered, for up to 2 days. Reheat them over medium heat in a dry nonstick frying pan or on a baking sheet in a 350°F oven.

VARIATION For vegetable pancakes, substitute 1 cup chopped shiitake mushrooms for the shrimp. You can also use other vegetables such as chopped asparagus or green beans, or shredded carrots or green bell pepper. Just avoid anything too wet or the pancakes won't crisp well.

Vietnamese-Style Sizzling Rice Crepes

SERVES 6 AS AN APPETIZER

I'll be honest here, this isn't the recipe to try on a Tuesday night after work. I felt strongly about including it, though, because it's delicious. And learning the recipe for these crepes (banh xeo) is important if you're looking to add interesting new gluten-free dishes to your repertoire. If you're feeling lazy (although it still takes some time), you can stuff the crepes with fresh herbs, bean sprouts, and a little shredded lettuce instead of the filling. The crisp edges of the hot crepes are part of the allure here; that means they really need to be cooked one at a time and eaten immediately. Make it a party in the kitchen—chat with friends, make a crepe, enjoy it with a gluten-free beer, and repeat!

1^1/$_2$ cups white rice flour

1^1/$_2$ teaspoons salt

^{1}/$_2$ teaspoon turmeric

2 cups cold water

^{1}/$_4$ cup unsweetened coconut milk

^{1}/$_2$ pound ground pork

2 cloves garlic, minced

1 tablespoon Asian fish sauce

1 teaspoon sugar

3 tablespoons vegetable oil, divided, plus more if needed

6 green onions, white and green parts, thinly sliced, divided

^{1}/$_2$ pound raw peeled shrimp, deveined and coarsely chopped

8 ounces bean sprouts

1 cup fresh cilantro leaves

1 cup fresh mint leaves

Nuoc cham (page 27), for serving

In a bowl, whisk together the rice flour, salt, turmeric, water, and coconut milk. Set aside.

Combine the pork, garlic, fish sauce, and sugar in a small bowl. In a 10-inch nonstick frying pan, heat 1 tablespoon of the oil over medium-high heat. Add the white parts of the green onion and cook for about 30 seconds. Add the pork mixture and cook, stirring occasionally, until it loses its pink color, about 5 minutes. Transfer the filling to a clean bowl. Return the pan to the heat. Add the shrimp and cook, stirring occasionally, until it loses its raw color, 2 to 3 minutes. Stir in the bean sprouts and cook until just starting to wilt, about 3 minutes longer. Add the shrimp and bean sprouts to the bowl with the pork and toss to combine. (The filling will keep, covered, in the refrigerator for up to 2 days.)

To cook the crepes, wipe the nonstick pan clean. Heat 1 teaspoon of the oil in the pan over medium-high heat. Stir the batter. Using a ^{1}/$_2$-cup measure, scoop out ^{1}/$_2$ cup of batter into the hot pan. Pick up the pan and swirl it in a circular motion to form a thin, round crepe. Return the pan to the heat and cook until the edges of the crepe look lacy and the top is partially cooked, about 2 minutes. Scoop about ^{1}/$_2$ cup of the filling onto the crepe. Cover the pan and lower the heat to medium. Cook until the edges of the crepe start to curl and

HEADS UP
The dish calls for *nuoc cham* (page 27). You can prepare it up to 2 weeks ahead.

the filling is hot, 2 to 3 minutes longer. Uncover the pan. If the edges of the crepe are not crisp, drizzle 1 teaspoon of oil around the outside of the crepe and continue cooking until crisp.

Transfer the crepe to a plate and top the filling with some of the cilantro, mint, and green onion tops. Fold the crepe in half so it looks like an omelet. Serve immediately with a drizzle of *nuoc cham*. Repeat the process, stirring the batter before each crepe, for a total of 6 crepes.

Steamed Rice Sheets *with Pork and Shrimp Filling*

 SERVES 4 TO 6 AS AN APPETIZER

The thought of making banh cuon, *or thin rice flour sheets, completely intimidated me at first. Traditional versions involve steaming the rice sheets one by one on a piece of cheesecloth carefully suspended over simmering water, a process that seemed fussy and difficult. The amazing Lucy Eklund, executive pastry chef of Jade: Bistro, Teahouse, & Patisserie in Portland, taught me how to make them in a nonstick pan with a tight-fitting lid. Although still time-consuming, this method is pretty straightforward. Just to be safe, you may want to double the batter the first time around as you work your way through the learning curve. I find the rice sheets work best using Erawan brand white rice flour. Use the dip-and-scoop method of measuring the flour and starches in this recipe, leveling off the top with a butter knife. Spooning the flour into the cup will not yield the same results.*

2/3 cup white rice flour (preferably Erawan brand)

2/3 cup tapioca flour (also called tapioca starch)

2 tablespoons cornstarch

1/2 teaspoon salt plus a pinch

2 1/2 cups water

2 tablespoons vegetable oil, divided, plus more for the pan

2 large shallots, thinly sliced

10 ounces ground pork

5 ounces raw shrimp, peeled and chopped

1/2 teaspoon freshly ground black pepper

Cilantro leaves, for serving

Cucumber matchsticks, for serving

Nuoc cham (page 27), for serving

In a bowl, combine the rice flour, tapioca flour, cornstarch, and a pinch of the salt. Slowly whisk in the water and 1 tablespoon of the oil until you have a very thin batter. Set aside.

In an 8- to 10-inch nonstick frying pan, heat 1 tablespoon of the oil over medium-high heat. Add the shallots and cook, stirring occasionally, until starting to brown, about 3 minutes. Add the ground pork and cook, breaking it up with a wooden spoon or a spatula, until it loses its pink color, about 3 minutes. Stir in the chopped shrimp, remaining 1/2 teaspoon salt, and pepper and continue cooking until the shrimp is pink in color, about 5 minutes. Transfer the filling to a bowl and wipe out the frying pan; make sure nothing is left in the pan. (The filling will keep, covered, in the refrigerator for up to 2 days. Reheat it before filling the rice sheets.)

To make the rice sheets, have a cutting board (preferably plastic) nearby for banging out and rolling the rice sheets; wipe a little vegetable oil on the surface to keep the rolls from sticking. Heat 1 teaspoon of oil in the frying pan over medium heat. Whisk the batter well to recombine the starches. Using a 1/4-cup measure, scoop out about 3 tablespoons of batter (the cup will be about three-quarters full) and add it to the hot pan.

HEADS UP
The dish calls for *nuoc cham*.
You can prepare it up to
2 weeks ahead.

Pick up the pan and swirl it in a circular motion to form a thin, round crepe. Pour any excess batter back into the bowl and return the pan to the heat. When the batter sets—this should only take seconds—cover the pan with a lid and steam until the top is cooked, 30 seconds to 1 minute. Loosen the edges of the rice sheet with a rubber spatula, if necessary. Pick up the pan and, in one quick motion, invert the pan and bang it on the cutting board so the rice sheet falls straight out. You want it to land flat; if the rice sheet bunches up it will be difficult to unfold. (A bit of bunching around the edges is okay, and there is extra batter in case, like me, you have a few larger mishaps.) If the rice sheet does bunch up, let it cool for a minute before trying to unfold it. The rice sheet will be white and springy; the texture will not be like a traditional crepe or pancake. Do not worry if there are a few small holes; it won't be noticeable when you roll up the filling.

Return the pan to the heat and repeat the process, whisking the batter well before adding it to the pan. Wipe the pan with an oiled paper towel after every 3 or 4 rice sheets. If the edges start to crisp, or there are multiple holes in the rice sheet from excessive bubbling, lower the heat to medium-low. While one rice sheet steams in the pan, fill the cooked one on the cutting board. Spoon 2 tablespoons of the filling into the center of the sheet, forming a horizontal log. Gently bring the lower part of the roll up over the filling to enclose it. Do not pull and stretch it or it will break. Fold in the sides over the filling and then roll into a cylinder. Press lightly to seal the edges. Transfer the roll to a plate.

When ready to serve, reheat the rolls in the microwave or on a plate, covered with foil, in a 300°F oven. Serve with cilantro, cucumbers, and a drizzle of *nuoc cham*. You will need to eat the rolls with a fork (or chopsticks); they are too delicate to pick up.

FIVE Noodles

If you've ever stood in the noodle aisle of an Asian market, the selection seems staggering, but once you become familiar with each noodle and its characteristics, the job becomes much more manageable. Lucky for you, being gluten free means you can eliminate half the choices right off the bat! Cross those wheat noodles and egg noodles (including ramen, udon, and somen) straight from the list. The remaining noodles—rice, cellophane, and 100 percent buckwheat soba—leave ample opportunity for you to get your noodle fix. This chapter includes recipes for each of these types, giving you a chance to get to know each noodle and how to work with it.

In addition to the Asian market, most of these noodles are becoming readily available in supermarkets. Every time I shop at a new market I check the Asian food aisle and almost always find at least one brand of rice noodles and one of cellophane noodles. Finding pure buckwheat soba still proves tricky, but it is available at health food stores and upscale groceries. All the recipes here call for dried noodles; although it is possible to find fresh rice noodles and soba noodles, the packages are often poorly labeled, if at all. Unless you have a highly reputable source for fresh noodles, I would use caution since they may contain wheat flour or wheat starch. When cooking Asian noodles, I like to rinse off any excess starch after draining them.

Many of the noodle dishes in this chapter serve four as a light main course. For a more substantial meal, start with an appetizer or add a side dish or two. You can also double the ingredients in the recipe, but cook the dish in two batches. These noodles generally don't perform well in an overcrowded pan.

GUIDE TO GLUTEN-FREE ASIAN NOODLES

Cellophane noodles (also called mung-bean noodles, glass noodles, bean threads, *sai fun*, and *harasume*): Made from the starch of mung beans, this vegetable-based noodle goes by many aliases. If the ingredient list says mung bean starch (and possibly another starch such as potato) and water, you've found the right noodle. The dried noodles are thin and white, but once cooked they are completely transparent (thus "glass" noodles). They have a delightful chewy, almost bouncy texture. Because they taste neutral on their own, cellophane noodles absorb their surrounding flavors, making them incredibly versatile.

In terms of size, I've seen whisper-thin cellophane noodles (similar to angel hair pasta) that I use for stuffing salad rolls or spring rolls, and ever-so-slightly thicker noodles (think thin spaghetti) that I use in stir-fries. Cellophane noodles need about a 15-minute soak in warm water before they're added to stir-fried or simmered dishes. After soaking the noodles, I usually cut them into smaller lengths with scissors. The size doesn't really matter (although 3 to 4 inches makes sense); you just want them to be manageable.

Also included in the cellophane noodle category is Korean *tangmyon*, made from sweet potato starch. The sweet potato noodles are generally a bit thicker than mung bean noodles, consequently taking a few minutes longer to cook. Although I love these noodles and prefer to use them in the recipe Sweet Potato Noodles with Beef and Vegetables (page 91), they are hard to find. If your plans don't include a trip to the Asian market, substitute mung bean noodles instead.

Rice noodles: These noodles are made from rice flour and water. Rice noodles come in many shapes and sizes, and often with a variety of possible names on the package labels. To avoid confusion, I suggest looking at the noodle itself (round versus flat, wide versus thin), along with the name on the package to determine what you need. I will suggest the appropriate size noodle for each recipe. For example, rice vermicelli is very thin, ranging from skeins of angel hair to a slightly larger and rounder thin spaghetti. The brittle noodles (known as *bun* in Vietnamese) need only a brief soak in just-boiled water to render them ready for business. Rice vermicelli forms a perfect bed for Vietnamese Rice Noodle Salad (page 84) and adds bulk to a batch of salad rolls.

Long, flat rice noodles, often called rice sticks, come in a few different widths, similar to choosing Italian pasta. For the Stir-Fried Rice Noodles with Chicken and Peanut Sauce (page 83) and the Red Curry Soup with Chicken and Rice Noodles (page 87), I like using a width similar to pad Thai noodles or linguine. Many sources suggest soaking the noodles before boiling them for a more even texture, though I haven't found that

Korean sweet potato *tangmyon* ↓

rice vermicelli ↑

←··· buckwheat soba

cellophane noodles ↑

rice sticks →

step necessary. If you do find a specific brand of noodles cooks unevenly, next time soak them in warm water for about 20 minutes before boiling. Regardless, rinse the noodles with cold water after you drain them to remove excess starch and keep them from forming one giant lump. (If they do end up clumping together, rinse them again in warm water right before you need them.) The noodles reheat quickly in a stir-fry or hot soup.

Soba noodles: Although soba noodles are made from buckwheat flour (a gluten-free grain), they often contain some wheat flour as well, making anything but the pure buckwheat versions off-limits. I love the toothsome organic 100 percent buckwheat soba noodles available at health food stores and upscale groceries. In fact, I almost never buy my soba noodles from an Asian market because the ingredients can be so easily lost in label translation. Many Japanese restaurants offer soba noodles on their menus, but remember to ask if they are entirely gluten free; chances are slim.

Soba noodles feel substantial in your mouth, probably due to the whole-grain goodness of buckwheat flour. The brown noodles have a hearty chew and a hint of nuttiness. Soba tastes great hot or chilled, but because the noodles have a distinctive flavor, I either keep the sauce super simple to highlight that flavor or go completely bold to stand right up to it. Soba noodles can be boiled and served (after a quick rinse to remove excess starch) or subsequently stir-fried, but they need no preliminary soaking.

Korean buckwheat noodles, known as *naengmyon*, allegedly combine buckwheat flour and sweet potato starch, though I have not seen a gluten-free brand even in specialty markets. Lacking a Korean translator, I would skip these and stick with the pure buckwheat soba noodles.

Other gluten-free noodles: In addition to my favorites listed above, you may come across gluten-free Asian noodles made from acorn starch, potato starch, tapioca, or kuzu root. Read the package for cooking instructions. With familiarity, you may be able to use these in place of cellophane noodles or rice noodles in some recipes.

In the refrigerated section, you might also find water-packed shirataki "noodles" or kelp "noodles". While these products are noodle shaped, texturally they are not good substitutes in any of the recipes here.

Stir-Fried Rice Noodles *with Chicken and Peanut Sauce*

 SERVES 4

I intended to include a recipe for classic pad Thai, but after tasting the combination of flavors in this recipe, I changed course. Use wider flat noodles (like those meant for pad Thai) as opposed to thin rice vermicelli, which would get tangled up in the sauce. Kids love this dish, though use your judgment on whether to lower the heat in the peanut sauce. The stir-fry comes together quickly, so make sure all your ingredients are ready to go, including the peanut sauce, before you start cooking.

8 ounces flat rice noodles

$1/2$ pound boneless skinless chicken breasts, cut crosswise into $1/4$-inch-thick slices and then into thin strips

2 teaspoons soy sauce or tamari GF

1 teaspoon ground coriander

$1/4$ teaspoon salt

2 tablespoons vegetable oil

1 carrot peeled and shredded (about $1/2$ cup)

4 green onions, white and green parts, thinly sliced

1 cup bean sprouts

1 cup Peanut Satay Sauce (page 31), plus more if needed

$1/4$ cup store-bought GF or homemade chicken broth (page 37), if needed

2 tablespoons freshly squeezed lime juice

2 tablespoons chopped fresh cilantro

2 tablespoons chopped peanuts

Cook the noodles in a large pot of boiling water until just done, about 5 minutes, or according to package directions. (Remove a noodle with tongs and taste it for doneness.) Drain the noodles in a colander and rinse with cold water to stop the cooking. Set the noodles aside until ready to use. In a small bowl, toss the chicken with the soy sauce, coriander, and salt. In a large frying pan or a wok, heat the oil over medium-high heat. Add the carrot and green onion and cook, stirring frequently, until wilted, about 1 minute. Add the chicken to the pan and cook, stirring occasionally, until cooked through, about 4 minutes.

Stir in the reserved noodles, bean sprouts, and peanut sauce. Toss everything together with tongs to combine and cook until heated through, 3 to 5 minutes. If the dish is not saucy enough for you, pour in a bit more peanut sauce or about $1/4$ cup chicken broth (or both). Stir in the lime juice. Serve the noodles hot, topped with the chopped cilantro and peanuts.

VARIATION Make a vegetarian version using extra-firm tofu instead of the chicken.

HEADS UP
The dish calls for peanut satay sauce (page 31). You can prepare it up to 1 week ahead.

Vietnamese Rice Noodle Salad

 SERVES 4

This hearty noodle salad makes a great party dish, perfect for a warm summer evening. Basically, you create your own noodle bowl—a bed of rice noodles topped with vegetables, the protein of your choice, fresh herbs, and a sprinkling of peanuts. Finish it off with a healthy dose of nuoc cham *and as much hot sauce as you like. You can choose any combination of vegetables you like, but I generally mix at least two or three types, including Carrot and Daikon Pickle (page 114) for tangy crunch.*

---

6 ounces thin rice vermicelli

3 cups shredded or thinly sliced mixed vegetables, such as cucumbers, lettuce, carrots, daikon radishes, Carrot and Daikon Pickle (page 114), or whole bean sprouts

Nuoc cham (page 27), divided

Roasted Pork Meatballs (page 47), Grilled Pork Satay (page 42), Lemongrass Shrimp Skewers (page 44), or other topping (see box)

1 cup lightly packed fresh cilantro and/or mint leaves

1/3 cup chopped roasted, unsalted peanuts

Sriracha or other chili-garlic sauce GF, for serving (optional)

Bring a large pot of water to a boil. Add the rice noodles. Remove the pan from the heat and let the noodles stand in the water until tender, 5 to 10 minutes depending on the thickness. Drain the noodles in a colander and then rinse with cold water. Squeeze any excess water from the noodles; transfer them to a large bowl. Add the vegetables to the bowl and toss with 1/2 cup of the *nuoc cham*. Transfer the noodles and vegetables to a serving platter.

Top the noodles with the roasted meatballs. Sprinkle with the herbs and peanuts. Pass additional *nuoc cham* at the table to spoon over each serving. (The *nuoc cham* is the major flavoring component, not just a dipping sauce in this case. Don't be afraid to add more.) Pass the hot sauce at the table.

> **TOPPINGS**
>
> The noodle salad is a general formula—noodles, vegetables, and protein—for you to play with. In addition to the meatballs, any of the following would feel right at home atop your noodles:
>
> Grilled Pork Satay (page 42)
> Lemongrass Shrimp Skewers (page 44)
> Grilled chicken from Korean-Style Chicken Tacos (page 49)
> Crispy Spring Rolls (page 52)
> Bulgogi (page 165)
>
> Almost any simply grilled or sautéed meat, shrimp, chicken, or tofu with an Asian flair will fit in just fine.

> **HEADS UP**
>
> This dish calls for one of many toppings. Note any advance preparation required for the toppings you choose. The dish calls for *nuoc cham*. You can prepare it up to 2 weeks ahead.

Red Curry Soup *with Chicken and Rice Noodles*

 SERVES 4

This curry soup, chock full of chicken, noodles, and a rich flavorful broth, makes a satisfying one-dish meal. Use the flat rice noodles similar to linguine (pad Thai noodles); thinner rice vermicelli may clump. If you plan on eating all the soup immediately, you can mix the noodles right into the broth; otherwise, keep them separate until you assemble the soup in the bowls. As the soup cools, the noodles will soak up every last bit of liquid, leaving you with some tasty noodles, but no broth.

8 ounces flat rice noodles

1 pound boneless, skinless chicken breasts, cut crosswise into thin slices and then into thin strips

2 tablespoons Asian fish sauce

2 tablespoons vegetable oil

1 small onion, thinly sliced

2 cloves garlic, minced

3 tablespoons red curry paste GF, such as Thai Kitchen

1/2 teaspoon turmeric

1/2 teaspoon ground coriander

3/4 teaspoon salt

2 (14-ounce) cans unsweetened coconut milk

2 cups store-bought GF or home-made chicken broth (page 37)

Cilantro leaves, for serving

Shredded cabbage, for serving

Lime wedges, for serving

Sriracha or other chili-garlic sauce GF, for serving

Cook the noodles in a large pot of boiling water until just done, about 5 minutes, or according to package directions. (Remove a noodle with tongs and taste it for doneness.) Drain the noodles in a colander and rinse with cold water to stop the cooking. Set the noodles aside until ready to use. In a small bowl, toss the chicken with the fish sauce. Let stand while you prepare the soup.

In a pot, heat the oil over medium heat. Add the onion and cook, stirring occasionally, until starting to brown, about 10 minutes. Stir in the garlic, curry paste, turmeric, and coriander and cook, stirring, for about 1 minute. Add the salt, coconut milk, and chicken broth and bring to a boil. Lower the heat and simmer, partially covered, to infuse the flavors, 10 to 15 minutes.

Add the chicken and fish sauce to the simmering broth. Continue cooking until the chicken is cooked through, about 5 minutes. To serve, divide the noodles among 4 bowls and ladle the soup over the noodles. Top with the cilantro, cabbage, a squeeze of lime juice, and hot sauce to taste.

VARIATION Brew up a delicious seafood curry soup: Instead of the chicken, add a pound of medium raw shrimp, bay scallops, crab, or a combination of these (tossed with the fish sauce) and simmer for 5 minutes.

Ants Climbing a Tree

 SERVES 4

At first I wasn't so sure about using the popular name for this Chinese noodle dish (I'm not a bugs-as-food kind of gal!), but after repeatedly enjoying the little nuggets of pork clinging to the slippery noodles for dear life, I was actually charmed by the image. I enjoy the bit of pork fat coating the noodles, but you can drain off the fat after cooking the pork if you prefer. This recipe makes a light main dish for four; serve it with Chilled Asparagus with Sesame Dressing (page 120) for a more filling meal. Or double the ingredients and cook it in two batches.

6 ounces cellophane (mung bean) noodles (sometimes called bean threads or sai fun)

12 ounces ground pork

2 tablespoons sake

3 tablespoons soy sauce **or** tamari **GF**, divided

2 tablespoons vegetable oil

4 cloves garlic, minced

1 teaspoon grated fresh ginger

6 green onions, white and green parts, thinly sliced, divided

4 teaspoons Chinese chile bean sauce **GF**, or substitute 1 tablespoon miso paste **GF** and 1¹/₂ teaspoons Sriracha

³/₄ cup store-bought **GF** or home-made chicken broth (page 37)

¹/₃ cup coarsely chopped fresh cilantro leaves

Freshly ground black pepper, for serving

Lemon wedges, for serving (optional)

Soak the noodles in a bowl of hot tap water until softened, about 15 minutes. (If you can stretch out a noodle and it bounces back, it's done.) Drain the noodles in a colander and then cut them into smaller lengths with scissors. In a small bowl, stir together the pork, sake, and 1 tablespoon of the soy sauce.

Heat the oil in a large frying pan or a wok over high heat. Add the garlic, ginger, and green onion whites and cook, stirring, until fragrant, about 20 seconds. Add the pork and cook, stirring occasionally, until it loses its pink color, about 5 minutes. Drain off the extra pork fat if you prefer. Stir in the chile bean sauce, noodles, the remaining 2 tablespoons soy sauce, and the chicken broth. Toss with tongs to combine and then simmer until the noodles are just tender and absorb most of the sauce, 3 to 5 minutes longer. Remove the pan from the heat and stir in the green onion tops and the cilantro. Serve topped with a bit of black pepper and a squeeze of lemon juice.

VARIATION You can use ground chicken or turkey instead of the pork.

Crabby Noodles *with Snow Peas*

 SERVES 4

Of all the benefits of living in Oregon, having friends who are willing to take you crabbing is probably the greatest. After a day at sea, when everyone has had their fill, I often have the enviable task of coming up with recipes to use all the extra crab. The simplicity of this stir-fry highlights the flavor of the crab. I like to use clam juice to finish cooking the noodles—it adds a pleasant, briny flavor—but chicken broth works, too. The snow peas add a perfect amount of crunch, but slice them thin so they aren't too intrusive. This recipes makes a light main dish for four. Serve it with Yakuza Cucumber and Avocado Salad (page 119) or double the ingredients and cook it in two batches.

6 ounces cellophane (mung bean) noodles (sometimes called bean threads or sai fun)

4 tablespoons vegetable oil, divided

6 green onions, white and green parts, thinly sliced

4 cloves garlic, minced

1/4 pound snow peas, cut diagonally into 1/4-inch-thick strips

1/2 pound cooked, picked crabmeat (do not use imitation crab; it often contains gluten)

1/2 cup bottled clam juice or substitute store-bought GF or homemade chicken broth (page 37)

2 tablespoons Asian fish sauce

1/3 cup chopped fresh cilantro

Soak the noodles in a bowl of hot tap water until softened, about 15 minutes. (If you can stretch out a noodle and it bounces back, it's done.) Thoroughly drain the noodles in a colander and cut them into smaller lengths with scissors.

Heat 2 tablespoons of the oil in a large frying pan or a wok over medium-high heat. Add the green onions and garlic and cook, stirring occasionally, for 1 minute. Add the snow peas and cook 1 minute longer. Add the remaining 2 tablespoons oil to the pan and then stir in the noodles and the crab. Toss with tongs to combine. Add the clam juice and fish sauce and simmer, turning the noodles occasionally, until the noodles are just tender and absorb most of the liquid, 3 to 5 minutes. Remove the pan from the heat and toss in the cilantro.

VARIATION Instead of crabmeat, use cooked baby shrimp or a combination of the two.

Seafood and Glass Noodle Casserole

 SERVES 4

The first time I tried koong ob woon sen, the dish appeared at the table in a darling single-serving clay casserole. As much as I would love to suggest this serving method at home, I know you would rather make one batch in the Dutch oven (or a wide pot) you already have in your kitchen. Assembling the dish is simple: layer the ingredients in the casserole—starting with the ever-flavorful bacon—get that bacon sizzling, and then give the whole thing a quick steam on the stove top. I really love the combination of crab and shrimp, but you can use all of one kind (or even scallops or cubed fish) if you prefer. This recipe makes a light main dish for four. Start with an appetizer or serve it with Bok Choy with Oyster Sauce (page 121).

---

5 to 6 ounces cellophane (mung bean) noodles (sometimes called bean threads or sai fun)

1 cup store-bought GF or home-made chicken broth (page 37)

3 tablespoons oyster sauce GF

2 tablespoons Asian fish sauce

1/4 pound thick-sliced bacon, cut crosswise into 1/2-inch-thick strips

1 tablespoon minced fresh ginger

6 green onions, white and green parts, thinly sliced

3 cloves garlic, minced

1/2 pound cooked, picked crabmeat (do not use imitation crab; it usually contains gluten)

1/2 pound medium raw shrimp, peeled and deveined

1/2 teaspoon freshly ground black pepper

1 1/2 teaspoons toasted sesame oil

1/2 cup fresh cilantro leaves

Soak the noodles in a bowl of hot tap water until softened, about 15 minutes. (If you can stretch out a noodle and it bounces back, it's done.) Drain the noodles in a colander and then rinse with cold water. Cut the noodles into smaller lengths with scissors. Meanwhile, combine the chicken broth, oyster sauce, and fish sauce in a bowl. Add the noodles and toss to coat.

Put the bacon in the bottom of a Dutch oven. Add the ginger, green onions, and garlic and then pour in the noodle mixture. Spoon the crabmeat over the noodles and top with the shrimp. Sprinkle in the black pepper and drizzle the shrimp with the sesame oil.

Set the Dutch oven over medium heat. When you hear the bacon start to sizzle, continue cooking for about 3 minutes and then cover the pot and lower the heat to medium-low. Cook until the noodles absorb the broth and the shrimp are opaque, 12 to 15 minutes. The shrimp should be pink when you peek under the lid. Add the cilantro and toss everything together with tongs before serving.

Sweet Potato Noodles *with Beef and Vegetables*

 SERVES 4

The playful combination of colors, flavors, and textures makes this a delightful dish (known as jap chae on Korean menus), and one of my personal favorites. The noodles, made from sweet potato starch, are chewy and neutral tasting, accommodating whatever sauce surrounds them. You can find them with the dried noodles in Asian markets, or substitute cellophane (mung bean) noodles if you prefer. This recipe includes only a small amount of marinated beef (bulgogi, page 165), so I've repeated the marinating instructions here. If you already have a batch on hand, though, you can use that. Serve the noodles with kimchi and a bowl of rice, or double the recipe for a larger one-dish meal.

---

2 tablespoons plus $^{1}/_{3}$ cup soy sauce or tamari GF, divided

$1^{1}/_{2}$ teaspoons plus $1^{1}/_{2}$ tablespoons toasted sesame oil, divided

2 teaspoons plus 2 tablespoons sugar, divided

1 teaspoon sake

8 ounces rib-eye steak, very thinly sliced (put the steak in the freezer for 20 minutes for easier slicing)

8 ounces sweet potato vermicelli

3 cloves garlic, minced

$^{1}/_{2}$ teaspoon freshly ground black pepper

2 tablespoons vegetable oil, divided

1 small onion, thinly sliced

1 small green bell pepper, thinly sliced

8 shiitake mushrooms, stems removed, caps thinly sliced

1 carrot, peeled and cut into matchstick strips

Salt

5 ounces fresh spinach (about 4 cups)

To make the *bulgogi*, combine 2 tablespoons of the soy sauce, $1^{1}/_{2}$ teaspoons of the sesame oil, 2 teaspoons of the sugar, and the sake in a small bowl. Mix well to combine. Put the meat in a glass baking dish or a gallon-size resealable bag. Add the marinade and toss to coat. Refrigerate the *bulgogi*, covered, for at least 1 hour or up to 24 hours. More time equals more flavor.

Soak the noodles in a bowl of hot tap water for 15 minutes. Drain the noodles in a colander. Cook the noodles in a large pot of boiling water until just done, 3 to 5 minutes, or according to package directions. (Remove a noodle with tongs and taste it for doneness.) Drain the noodles in a colander and rinse with cold water to stop the cooking. Using scissors, cut the noodles into approximately 4-inch lengths. Transfer the noodles to a large bowl.

To make the sauce, in a small bowl, stir together the remaining $^{1}/_{3}$ cup soy sauce, $1^{1}/_{2}$ tablespoons sesame oil, 2 tablespoons sugar, and the garlic and black pepper. Set aside.

To cook the vegetables, heat 1 tablespoon of the vegetable oil in a large frying pan or a wok over medium-high heat. Add the onion, pepper, and mushrooms and cook, stirring occasionally, for 3 minutes. Add the carrot and a pinch of salt and cook, stirring occasionally, until the carrots are tender but still

(continued)

(continued from page 91)

HEADS UP
You'll need to marinate the
meat for at least 1 hour and up
to 24 hours.

crisp, about 3 minutes longer. Stir the sauce, then add all but 1 tablespoon of the sauce to the pan. Set aside the remaining sauce. Toss the vegetables a few times to coat and then transfer them to the bowl with the noodles. Toss well to combine.

In the same pan, heat the remaining 1 tablespoon vegetable oil over medium-high heat. Add the spinach and cook until wilted, about 2 minutes. Add a pinch of salt and the remaining 1 tablespoon sauce. Transfer the spinach to the bowl with the noodles.

To cook the meat, heat the same pan over medium-high heat. Add the meat to the pan and cook the *bulgogi*, turning occasionally, until brown and cooked through, about 5 minutes. Transfer the meat to the bowl with the noodles. Toss everything together until well combined. Serve warm or at room temperature.

VARIATIONS Substitute cellophane noodles for the sweet potato noodles. They will cook slightly faster, in about 3 minutes.

Use ground beef instead of the rib eye, or eliminate the meat for a vegetarian version.

Chilled Tangy Soba Noodles

 SERVES 2 AS A MAIN DISH, 4 AS A SIDE DISH

Both Korean and Japanese cuisines offer versions of cold soba noodles accompanied by either a chilled broth or a dead-simple dipping sauce. Traditional soba noodle making is a craft, and so the simplicity of the sauce highlights the taste and texture of the noodle instead of masking it. In my opinion, commercial brands of soba made from 100 percent buckwheat flour don't have quite the right texture to stand alone in broth, but I do like this Korean-inspired version, swathed in a tangy, sweet, and hot sauce. The egg wedges are an integral part of the dish; they add protein and an interesting counterpoint to the bite of the noodle. Because the dish is so simple (and pure buckwheat soba can be expensive), it's best suited as a main dish for two or a side dish for more.

1 (7- to 8-ounce) package 100 percent buckwheat soba noodles **GF**

2 cloves garlic, minced

2 tablespoons soy sauce or tamari **GF**

1¹/₂ tablespoons unseasoned rice vinegar

1 tablespoon Korean chili powder, or substitute 1 tablespoon paprika mixed with ¹/₄ teaspoon cayenne pepper

1 tablespoon sugar

1¹/₂ teaspoons toasted sesame oil

¹/₂ English cucumber, halved lengthwise, seeded, and cut into matchstick strips

1 tablespoon toasted sesame seeds

2 hard-cooked eggs, each cut into 4 wedges

Cook the noodles in a large pot of boiling water until just done, about 8 minutes, or according to package directions. (Remove a noodle with tongs and taste it for doneness.) Drain the noodles in a colander and rinse with cold water to stop the cooking. Transfer the noodles to a bowl and chill them in the refrigerator until very cold, 2 to 3 hours. Alternatively, for faster chilling, add cold water and a handful of ice cubes to the bowl of noodles; let stand for 20 to 30 minutes, then drain.

While the noodles chill, whisk together the garlic, soy sauce, vinegar, chili powder, sugar, and sesame oil in a small bowl. When ready to serve, toss the noodles with the sauce.

For serving, divide the noodles between 2 large plates. Sprinkle the cucumber matchsticks and sesame seeds over the top. Surround the noodles with wedges of egg and serve immediately while the noodles are cold.

HEADS UP

The noodles need to chill for at least 20 minutes and up to several hours.

Soba Noodles *with Stir-Fried Shiitake Mushrooms*

 SERVES 4

Shiitake mushrooms pair well with soba noodles; the combination makes for a satisfying, savory vegetarian meal. Asparagus brings a bright spring flair to the dish, but it's just as delicious with wintery sliced cabbage. Look for 100 percent buckwheat soba at natural foods markets or upscale grocers. This recipe makes a light main dish for four. Serve it with Chilled Tofu with Cucumber Sunomono (page 129), or double the ingredients and cook in two batches.

1 (7- to 8-ounce) package 100 percent buckwheat soba noodles **GF**

2 tablespoons vegetable oil

1 small onion, thinly sliced

8 ounces shiitake mushrooms, stems removed, caps thinly sliced

6 ounces asparagus, cut diagonally into $\frac{1}{2}$-inch slices (about 1 cup)

$\frac{1}{4}$ cup soy sauce or tamari **GF**

2 tablespoons sake

$\frac{1}{8}$ teaspoon red pepper flakes

1 teaspoon toasted sesame oil

$\frac{1}{4}$ cup chopped fresh cilantro

$\frac{1}{2}$ teaspoon freshly ground black pepper

Cook the noodles in a large pot of boiling water until just done, about 8 minutes, or according to package directions. (Remove a noodle with tongs and taste it for doneness.) Drain the noodles in a colander and rinse with cold water to stop the cooking. Set aside.

Heat the oil over medium-high heat in a large frying pan or a wok. Add the onion and mushrooms and cook, stirring occasionally, until well browned, about 10 minutes. Add the asparagus and cook, stirring, about 2 minutes longer. Stir in the noodles, soy sauce, sake, and red pepper flakes. Toss with tongs until heated through, 2 to 3 minutes. Top the noodles with the sesame oil, cilantro, and black pepper.

VARIATION For a hearty winter version, substitute 3 cups shredded Napa cabbage for the asparagus.

SIX **Rice**

It may not be possible for me to adequately convey my feelings about rice, an ingredient unparalleled in the lexicon of gluten-free essentials. Aside from the obvious fact that billions of people count rice as their primary staple, Asian cooks take it one step further, creating innovative ways of using rice to every last bit of its potential. For someone following a gluten-free lifestyle, this opens some doors that may have temporarily closed. From rice comes noodles, pancakes, dumplings, mochi, crepes, rice paper wrappers, crackers, chewy Korean rice sticks, and sweet or savory cakes, not to mention that basic bowl of steamed grains. My pantry always houses at least ten kinds of rice (not necessarily all Asian), each with a distinct flavor and unique role in my cooking. If rice is something you toss on the side of the plate without a second thought, explore its possibilities. Embrace rice, sample different varieties, learn to cook it. And if it seems scary, buy a rice cooker; households throughout Asia consider them kitchen fixtures—perfect rice is as easy as pushing a button.

The most important thing to remember about rice is that all rice is not created equal. Its shape, size, and starch content all affect what ends up on your plate. You can purchase rice from a new crop or find some that has been sitting on the store shelf for ages. Older rice absorbs water at a different rate from new crop (a trait some cooks prefer); general guidelines are suggested in the recipes, but you may need to adjust water amounts slightly based on the reaction of your rice. Look at package directions as well. Asian markets offer a stunning number of imported and domestic types of rice, but lately many of my favorite brands are popping up in grocery stores, too. Look in the Asian aisle or along with the other types of rice. I list some rice basics below, but if you are interested in a deeper exploration, I highly recommend Jeffrey Alford and Naomi Duguid's captivating book, *Seductions of Rice*.

A GUIDE TO RICE

Jasmine rice: A long-grain, aromatic rice predominantly used in Thai and Vietnamese cooking. Once cooked, the grains remain distinct.

Medium-grain rice: A staple on Japanese and Korean tables, this rice is shorter and clumps together a bit more when cooked. It generally requires less water for cooking. After rinsing the rice, soak it for 20 minutes or so before cooking to yield a more toothsome texture. Excellent "Japanese-style" rice is produced in California, including several of my favorite brands: Nishiki, Tamaki, and Kokuho Rose.

Sticky rice (also called sweet rice, glutinous rice, or waxy rice): Don't be alarmed by the word "glutinous," which refers to the sticky texture; the rice does not contain gluten. Available in either long or short grain, sticky rice appears white when raw and translucent when cooked. Unlike jasmine and medium-grain rice, which are cooked using the absorption method, sticky rice must be soaked in water for several hours—a critical step to ensure even cooking—and then steamed over a raging pot of boiling water. Used in both savory and sweet preparations, the rice is sticky enough to roll into a ball and pick up with your hands. The sticky rice acts as a utensil, soaking up sauce or scooping up small bites of food. Japanese mochi comes from sticky rice, as does one of my favorite desserts, Mango with Sweet Rice and Coconut Sauce (page 187).

Sushi rice: You can purchase rice labeled "sushi rice," or use Japanese-style short- or medium-grain rice. Once cooked, mix the warm rice with a combination of rice vinegar, sugar, and salt (Sushi Rice, page 100).

Sweet rice flour (also called glutinous rice flour or sticky rice flour): Flour ground from grains of sticky rice. Use this flour for dumplings, dough, steamed cakes, and mochi. Do not confuse it with white rice flour; they have completely different properties. Because Thai and American brands are somewhat different, the recipes will indicate whether you need to use a specific kind.

White rice flour: Flour ground from long-grain rice. Uses include noodles, pancakes, crepes, rice sheets, dumplings, rice crackers, and sweet and savory cakes. Do not confuse it with sweet rice flour; they have completely different properties. Thai brands of rice flour are more finely ground and less grainy than American rice flours, resulting in a smoother-textured final product. Recipes will indicate whether a Thai brand is essential or not.

Korean rice cakes (also called rice sticks or *dduk*): One of my favorite foods on the planet, these "cakes," made from rice flour and water, are chewy, toothsome, and delicious. They come in two shapes, either 3-inch-long cylinders or flat ovals, the type I use in Stir-Fried Rice Cakes with Shrimp and Vegetables (page 110). Because they are only available at Asian markets (refrigerated or frozen), I limited the recipes to one, but urge you to pick some up if you have a chance. Soak rice cakes in cold water for about an hour before cooking.

Rice paper wrappers (also called spring roll wrappers or spring roll skins): Thin brittle rounds (or triangles) made from rice flour, or a combination of rice flour and tapioca flour, and water. Used to wrap salad rolls and spring rolls; you must first rehydrate the rice paper in water to soften it before folding it around the filling. Enjoy the pleasantly chewy texture as is, or deep-fry them into crisp submission.

Steamed Jasmine Rice

 SERVES 4 TO 6

The moisture content of rice varies depending on the brand and how long it sits on grocery store shelves. This ratio of rice to water almost always works well, but a few simple tricks will keep you on course. If your rice is still a little wet when it comes time for steaming, drape a clean dishtowel over the pot and cover with the lid. The towel helps absorb some of the excess liquid. If the rice seems dry before steaming, add 1 to 2 tablespoons water before replacing the lid. And don't forget to save leftovers; they're perfect for fried rice.

2 cups jasmine rice

2¹/₂ cups water

Put the rice in a bowl and cover it with cool water. Swish the rice around in the water with your hand until the liquid turns a milky color. Pour off the water and repeat the process until the water stays mostly clear, about three or four times. Drain the rice in a colander and then transfer it to a medium pot.

Add the water to the pot and bring to a boil. Let the water boil for about 1 minute and then cover the pot. Lower the heat to low and simmer until the rice is tender, about 15 minutes. Remove the pan from the heat. Uncover the pot and fluff the rice with a fork or a spatula. Replace the lid and let the rice steam for 5 minutes longer before serving.

Sushi Rice

 SERVES 4 TO 6

When you order sushi in a restaurant, the fish comes draped over rice that is seasoned with vinegar, sugar, and salt. Sushi rice is super easy to make at home and can be used as the foundation for a fun, interactive family dinner. Mound the sushi rice in bowls and set out a variety of toppings (Sushi Rice Bowl, page 107), or pick up some sheets of nori and make your own sushi rolls.

2 cups sushi rice or other medium- or short-grain rice

2$^{1}/_{3}$ cups water

$^{1}/_{4}$ cup unseasoned rice vinegar

2 tablespoons sugar

1$^{1}/_{2}$ teaspoons salt

Put the rice in a bowl and cover it with cool water. Swish the rice around in the water with your hand until the liquid turns a milky color. Pour off the water and repeat the process until the water stays mostly clear, about three or four times. Drain the rice in a colander and transfer it to a medium pot. Add the water and let the rice stand for about 15 minutes before cooking. Bring to a boil. Lower the heat to low and cook the rice, covered, for 15 minutes. Turn off the heat and let the rice steam, covered, for 10 minutes longer.

Meanwhile, combine the vinegar, sugar, and salt in a small saucepan. Bring to a boil and cook, stirring, until the sugar and salt dissolve, about 1 minute. Remove the pan from the heat and let cool to room temperature. (The seasoned vinegar can be made ahead. Refrigerate it, covered, for up to 1 week.)

Transfer the cooked rice to a large bowl. Slowly pour the vinegar mixture over the rice, using a spatula to gently fold them together. Cover the bowl with a barely damp cloth so the rice does not dry out. Serve warm or at room temperature. Do not refrigerate the cooked rice or it will end up crunchy.

Sticky Rice

 SERVES 4

My kids love sticky rice because you can roll it up in little balls and eat it with your hands. Because of the long soaking time, I used to think making it sounded like a pain. But as long as you think ahead, the cooking is actually more foolproof and easier to clean up than regular rice. It can be a little tricky to find—an Asian market will be your best bet—but try it once and see how you like it.

Sticky rice goes by many names. If that's not the one on the label, look for "sweet rice" or the unfortunately named "glutinous rice." (The rice does not contain gluten; "glutinous" refers to its sticky texture.) I assume you don't have a traditional Thai bamboo conical steamer around the house—neither do I—but any old steamer will work. Just make sure the rice does not touch the water.

---

2 cups sticky rice (also called sweet rice or glutinous rice)

HEADS UP
You'll need to soak the rice in water for at least 3 hours and up to 24 hours.

Put the rice in a bowl and cover it by at least 2 inches with cold water. Let the rice soak for at least 8 hours and up to 24 hours. A longer soaking time brings out more flavor in the rice, but for a quicker soak, cover the rice with warm water for at least 3 or 4 hours.

Bring several inches of water to boil in a large pot or a wok. Line a steamer tray or a colander (one that will fit in the pot) with cheesecloth or a thin, clean kitchen towel. Over the sink, pour the rice and soaking water into the colander. Fold the excess cheesecloth or towel over the rice. When the water has drained, transfer the colander to the pot of boiling water. The rice should not touch the water. If it does, set the colander on a small round rack in the bottom of the pan or elevate it using a scrunched round of aluminum foil. Cover the pot with a lid and steam until the rice is shiny and tender, about 25 minutes. Taste a piece of rice and if it is not yet tender, cover the pot and continue steaming until it is done. Transfer the rice to a bowl and break it up slightly using a spatula. Cover the bowl with a barely damp cloth so the rice does not dry out. Serve warm or at room temperature. Do not refrigerate the cooked rice or it will end up crunchy.

Coconut Rice

 SERVES 4

I use steamed jasmine or medium-grain rice as a neutral complement when I'm serving something saucy, but I turn to coconut rice as a tasty dish in its own right. For simpler meals, like some of the grilled skewers in chapter 3, the coconut rice adds a creamy, flavorful component. Personally, I would toss in all the optional toppings, but my kids prefer it plain. I compromise by setting the toppings out for any takers.

1¹/₂ cups jasmine rice

1 (14-ounce) can unsweetened coconut milk

¹/₂ cup water

1¹/₄ teaspoons salt

¹/₄ cup chopped fresh cilantro (optional)

Chopped green onion, green parts only (optional)

3 tablespoons shredded unsweetened coconut, toasted (optional)

Put the rice in a bowl and cover it with cool water. Swish the rice around in the water with your hand until the liquid turns a milky color. Pour off the water and repeat the process until the water stays mostly clear, about three or four times. Drain the rice in a colander and transfer it to a saucepan.

Add the coconut milk, water, and salt to the pan and bring to a boil over medium heat. Let it boil for about 1 minute and then cover the pot. Lower the heat to low and simmer until the rice is tender, about 15 minutes. Remove the pan from the heat. Uncover the pot and fluff the rice with a fork or a spatula. Replace the lid and let the rice steam for 5 minutes before serving. Stir in the cilantro, green onion, and coconut or serve alongside the rice.

Kimchi Fried Rice

 SERVES 4 TO 6

Because the addition of the kimchi makes this fried rice taste so unique, serve it as a side dish with something simple like grilled steak or chicken. Or top each serving with a fried egg for more of a meal. I use medium- or short-grain rice here (the flavor is more neutral than jasmine), precooked and chilled for best results.

¹/₄ pound thick-sliced uncured bacon, cut into ¹/₂-inch pieces

6 green onions, white and green parts, thinly sliced

1 to 2 tablespoons vegetable oil, if needed

3 cups cooked and chilled medium-grain rice

1 cup chopped kimchi **GF** with 1 tablespoon of its liquid

1 teaspoon soy sauce or tamari **GF**

1 teaspoon toasted sesame oil

In a large frying pan or a wok, cook the bacon over medium heat until starting to crisp. Add the green onions and cook, stirring, for 30 seconds. If there is less than 2 tablespoons of bacon fat in the pan, add the vegetable oil to make it 2 tablespoons. Increase the heat to medium-high.

Add the rice and cook, stirring occasionally, for 2 minutes. Stir in the kimchi and its liquid and cook, stirring occasionally, until everything is heated through, about 2 minutes longer. Add the soy sauce and sesame oil and serve hot or at room temperature.

VARIATIONS Instead of bacon, substitute ¹/₄ pound ground pork, ground beef, diced chicken, shrimp, tempeh (read the label to make sure it is gluten free), or firm tofu. Without the bacon, you need to add the 2 tablespoons of oil.

Spring Vegetable Fried Rice

 SERVES 4 TO 6

Fried rice hits the spot as a simple side dish or even a low-key meal. Start with cold, cooked rice (I use jasmine rice, but any kind will do) so the grains absorb less oil and keep from clumping together. It's easy enough to keep cooked rice on hand, but you can also order an extra quart of rice next time you get takeout and refrigerate it for later. I really prefer using a wok for fried rice because the vegetables get nice and charred, but a large nonstick pan works fine, too.

2 tablespoons plus 1 teaspoon vegetable oil, divided

2 eggs, beaten with a pinch of salt

1 tablespoon grated fresh ginger

4 green onions, white and green parts, thinly sliced

1 tablespoon chopped jalapeño chile

1 carrot, peeled and finely diced

1/2 pound asparagus, ends trimmed, spears cut diagonally into 3/4-inch slices

1/4 pound snow peas, cut diagonally into 3/4-inch slices (about 1 cup)

3 cups cooked and chilled jasmine rice

1/2 teaspoon salt

2 tablespoons soy sauce or tamari GF

1/2 teaspoon toasted sesame oil

In a large nonstick frying pan or a wok, heat 1 teaspoon of the vegetable oil over medium-high heat. Add the eggs and cook, stirring occasionally, until scrambled, about 1 minute. Transfer the eggs to a bowl. Heat 1 tablespoon of the vegetable oil over high heat. Add the ginger, green onions, and jalapeño and cook, stirring, until fragrant, about 30 seconds. Add the carrot, asparagus, and snow peas and cook, stirring occasionally, until lightly charred, about 2 minutes.

Add the remaining 1 tablespoon vegetable oil to the pan. Stir in the rice and egg and cook, stirring occasionally, until heated through, about 3 minutes. Add the salt, soy sauce, and sesame oil and mix well to combine. Serve hot or at room temperature.

VARIATIONS Fried rice is a perfect vehicle for using up leftover bits of meat. If you have a small amount of Chinese barbecued pork (page 169), *bulgogi* (page 165), chicken, or shrimp (1/2 to 1 cup chopped), toss it in along with the vegetables.

Sushi Rice Bowl

 SERVES 4 AS A MAIN DISH

Don't like sushi, you say? Well don't turn the page just yet. You don't have to use raw fish, or really any fish at all, for a sushi rice bowl. I listed spicy tuna in the ingredient list because it's my favorite, but I generally set out multiple toppings so each family member can create his or her own combination. Choose a single favorite (smoked salmon and asparagus) or a wide variety (see chart), using less of each if you opt for several toppings.

---

1 pound very fresh tuna steak or salmon fillet, cut into ¹/₂-inch dice

¹/₃ cup Super Secret Spicy Sauce (page 32), plus more to taste

Sushi rice (page 100)

2 cups shredded carrots and/or cucumber matchsticks

1 tablespoon toasted sesame seeds

Toss the tuna with the spicy sauce and keep refrigerated until ready to use. Scoop a serving of warm sushi rice into each of four serving bowls. Top with the spicy tuna, shredded carrots, cucumbers, and sesame seeds.

VARIATIONS Use this recipe as an opportunity for a fun, interactive family meal. Think of the ingredients in your favorite sushi rolls and give those a whirl. Or combine items from each category and create your own masterpiece.

> **HEADS UP**
> The recipe calls for several ingredients to be prepared ahead:
> The sushi rice, spicy sauce, and pickled ginger.

PROTEIN (³/₄ TO 1 POUND):
Cooked shrimp, salmon, or tuna
Smoked trout or salmon
Crabmeat tossed with a little mayonnaise (don't use imitation crabmeat; it often contains gluten)
Sushi-grade raw fish, such as salmon or tuna
Tofu tossed with Super Secret Spicy Sauce (page 32) and a squeeze of lemon juice
Omelet, cut into strips

VEGETABLES (3 CUPS):
Shredded carrots or radishes
Sliced green onions or cucumber matchsticks
Diced avocado
Blanched and sliced asparagus
Sautéed shiitake mushrooms
Blanched spinach with a dash of sesame oil

TOPPINGS:
Pickled ginger **GF** (page 35)
Wasabi **GF**
Toasted sesame seeds
Sliced fresh chiles
Soy sauce or tamari **GF**
Toasted sesame oil
Super Secret Spicy Sauce (page 32)
Toasted nori strips

Bibimbap

SERVES 4 AS A MAIN DISH

If your kids aren't familiar with the joys of Korean food, this is a great basic dish to pique their interest. Traditionally, small mounds of individual vegetable and meat toppings rest atop a serving of hot rice. Since each topping is a unique color, keeping them separate makes for a beautiful presentation. There are a lot of steps to the recipe (all of them easy), so I mix all the toppings together in one bowl to save time—and dishes. The rice and toppings make a great base, but it's the extras that really pull the dish together—I like mine with a fried egg on top (leave the yolk a bit runny to make a sauce), and I pass hot sauce, soy sauce GF*, and sesame oil at the table. The recipe includes only a small amount of marinated beef (bulgogi, page 165), so I've included the instructions here, but if you already have a batch on hand, or in the freezer, you can use that instead.*

2 tablespoons plus 2 teaspoons soy sauce or tamari GF, divided, plus more for serving

2¹/4 teaspoons toasted sesame oil, divided, plus more for serving

2 teaspoons sugar

1 teaspoon sake

¹/4 teaspoon freshly ground black pepper

8 ounces boneless rib-eye steak, very thinly sliced (put the steak in the freezer for 20 minutes for easier slicing)

4 ounces bean sprouts

Salt

10 ounces spinach, large stems removed

1 tablespoon vegetable oil

1 zucchini, cut into approximately 3¹/2 by ¹/4-inch strips

1 carrot, peeled and cut into matchstick strips or shredded

1 clove garlic, minced

In a small bowl, combine 2 tablespoons of the soy sauce, 1¹/2 teaspoons of the sesame oil, the sugar, sake, and black pepper. Mix well to combine. Put the meat in a glass baking dish or a gallon-size resealable bag. Add the marinade and toss to coat. Refrigerate the *bulgogi*, covered, for at least 1 hour or up to 24 hours. More time equals more flavor.

Bring a pot of water to a boil. Add the bean sprouts and cook for 1 minute. Remove the sprouts with a slotted spoon (keeping the water boiling) and drain them in a colander. Toss with a pinch of salt, ¹/4 teaspoon of the sesame oil, and 1 teaspoon of the soy sauce. Transfer the bean sprouts to a bowl.

Add the spinach to the boiling water and cook until wilted, about 1 minute. Drain the spinach well in the colander. When cool enough to handle, squeeze the excess liquid from the spinach. Toss the spinach with the remaining 1 teaspoon soy sauce, ¹/4 teaspoon of the sesame oil, and a pinch of salt. Add the spinach to the bowl with the bean sprouts.

In a large frying pan, heat the vegetable oil over medium-high heat. Add the zucchini, carrot, and garlic and cook until crisp-tender, about 3 minutes. Stir in a pinch of salt and the remaining ¹/4 teaspoon sesame oil. Transfer the vegetables to

4 cups steamed medium-grain rice

4 fried eggs, for serving (optional)

Chinese chile bean sauce GF, for serving, or substitute 2 parts miso paste GF mixed with 1 part Sriracha sauce

Shredded, roasted nori, for serving (optional)

HEADS UP

The meat will need to marinate for at least 1 hour and up to 24 hours.

the bowl. (The vegetables can be kept at room temperature, covered, for a few hours.)

Cut the meat crosswise into thin strips. Heat the same frying pan over medium-high heat. Cook the *bulgogi*, turning occasionally, until brown and cooked through, about 5 minutes. Transfer the meat to the bowl with the vegetables. Toss to combine.

For serving, divide the rice among 4 bowls. Top each serving of rice with some of the vegetables and meat. Top with a fried egg. Pass the sesame oil, soy sauce, chile bean sauce, and shredded nori at the table.

VARIATIONS Thinly sliced chicken breast works well in place of the beef, but cut the cooking time to about 3 minutes for very thin slices. You can leave meat out completely for a satisfying vegetarian version.

Stir-Fried Rice Cakes *with Shrimp and Vegetables*

 SERVES 4

Rice cakes are one of my favorite ingredients in the universe. No, not the dry crackerlike things you use for peanut butter, but the flat ovals of rice flour and water found in the refrigerator case (or freezer) at Asian markets. (The rice cakes are Korean in origin, but seem to be available in most Asian markets.) Soak the rice cakes in cold water to rehydrate them before tossing them in a stir-fry to keep the cooking time fast. Once you open a bag of rice cakes, use the remainder within 1 week or freeze them for longer storage. Be sure to use sliced rice cakes as opposed to the larger, cylindrical type.

1/2 pound medium raw shrimp, peeled and deveined

2 cloves garlic, minced

1 1/2 teaspoons toasted sesame oil, divided

2 tablespoons soy sauce or tamari **GF**

2 tablespoons sugar

1 1/2 tablespoons Chinese chile bean sauce **GF**, or substitute

1 tablespoon miso paste **GF** mixed with 1 1/2 teaspoons Sriracha sauce

1/4 cup water

1/4 teaspoon freshly ground black pepper

12 ounces sliced rice cakes, also called *dduk* (see page 12), soaked in cold water for 1 hour

2 tablespoons vegetable oil

1 small onion, diced

1/4 pound mushrooms, quartered

1 small zucchini, quartered lengthwise, then cut crosswise into 1/2-inch slices

1 carrot, peeled and cut into matchstick strips

In a small bowl, toss the shrimp with the garlic and 1/2 teaspoon of the sesame oil. In another small bowl, combine the remaining 1 teaspoon sesame oil, soy sauce, sugar, chile bean sauce, water, and black pepper. Drain the rice cakes in a colander and let stand until ready to use. The rice cakes will still feel very firm, but will soften as they cook.

In a large frying pan or a wok, heat the vegetable oil over medium-high heat. Add the onion and mushrooms and cook, stirring occasionally, until starting to brown, about 3 minutes. Stir in the zucchini and the shrimp and cook 2 minutes longer. Stir in the rice cakes, carrot, and soy sauce mixture. Simmer, stirring occasionally, until the rice cakes are cooked through and the sauce thickens, about 5 minutes. Serve hot.

VARIATIONS Kids love rice cakes, but this particular recipe is a bit spicy. To lower the heat, instead of the chile bean sauce, use the miso variation with just a touch of Sriracha sauce.

Instead of shrimp, use 1/2 pound marinated *bulgogi* (page 165).

The shrimp and vegetable stir-fry is delicious even without the rice cakes. Add some cooked rice noodles in their place or just keep it saucy and serve over steamed rice.

HEADS UP
The rice cakes will need to soak for 1 hour.

SEVEN Vegetables and Tofu

Vegetables bring such vibrancy to the table, adding color, texture, and a wide spectrum of flavors. And considering they're not only healthy but also inherently gluten free, I don't feel a tinge of guilt about strewing them willy-nilly over my dinner plate. In my efforts to share as much vegetable goodness as possible, I introduce them in many forms: pickles, salads, side dishes, and paired with tofu as a main course.

Pickling is one of my favorite ways to enjoy vegetables, providing crunch and a raw burst of flavor and acidity. The Carrot and Daikon Pickle, Cucumber Relish, and Cabbage Kimchi recipes in this chapter fit the bill, providing textural contrast and a tart spark when that's what is needed in a dish. They also make a light snack alongside a bowl of rice.

The side dishes offer a number of different vegetables in tasty, gluten-free sauces. Once you familiarize yourself with the techniques, you can replicate the recipes with other vegetables you enjoy. I was hard-pressed to find one I didn't love with the Sweet Miso Glaze (page 28)!

As an integral part of Asian cooking, tofu demands more respect than floating aimlessly in a cup of miso soup. The soybean-based curd provides an inexpensive, high-quality source of protein, perfect for those on a budget or looking to cut back on consumption of animal protein. Tofu's jack-of-all-trades identity keeps it successful in hot and cold dishes alike, and the curd proudly lives up to its reputation of soaking up the flavorful sauces that surround it. In its most basic form, tofu comes in several textures (silken, soft, firm, extra firm) and each recipe specifies which type to use. When you want to maintain tofu's shape and structure—such as when you sauté it—remove all the excess moisture first by setting drained cubes of tofu on paper towels. Let them stand for several minutes to remove that last bit of liquid, changing the towels if they get too wet. Look for tofu in the refrigerator case or in a shelf-stable aseptic pack.

Carrot and Daikon Pickle

 SERVES 4

Pickled vegetables often appear at the Vietnamese table; their crispness and acidity act as a counterpoint to many savory dishes, adding a hit of freshness just where you need it. I find the pickle an essential part of a Vietnamese Rice Noodle Salad (page 84), or right at home tucked in a lettuce leaf alongside Roasted Pork Meatballs (page 47). It can even stand on its own as a sweet-and-sour salad.

$^1/_2$ **pound carrots, peeled and cut into matchstick strips (about 2 cups)**

$^1/_2$ **pound daikon radish, peeled and cut into matchstick strips (about 2 cups)**

1 tablespoon salt

3 tablespoons sugar

$^1/_4$ **cup hot water**

$^1/_2$ **cup unseasoned rice vinegar**

HEADS UP
The pickle will need to marinate for at least 2 hours before serving.

Combine the carrot and radish in a colander set over an empty bowl or the sink. Sprinkle with salt, rubbing it into the vegetables with your fingers. Let the vegetables stand until they shed some of their liquid, about 20 minutes.

Meanwhile, in a bowl large enough to hold the vegetables, combine the sugar and the hot water and stir until the sugar dissolves. Stir in the vinegar. Squeeze the vegetables to remove any excess liquid and then add them to the bowl. Let the vegetables marinate for at least 2 hours, stirring occasionally. The pickle will keep in its liquid, covered, in the refrigerator for up to 3 days.

Thai Cucumber Relish

 SERVES 4

The light, refreshing nature of this cucumber relish makes me think summer, but you can certainly enjoy it any time of year. Sweet-and-tangy cucumbers pair perfectly with grilled Halibut Satay skewers (page 43), or they can accompany any dish that needs a tart little crunch. The relish even works as a simple salad.

³/₄ cup unseasoned rice vinegar

¹/₂ cup sugar

¹/₂ cup water

1¹/₂ teaspoons salt

2 English cucumbers, halved lengthwise, seeded, and thinly sliced crosswise

1 red jalapeño chile (or more to taste), thinly sliced

¹/₄ cup chopped fresh cilantro

HEADS UP
You'll need to chill the pickling liquid for at least 20 minutes.

In a small saucepan, bring the vinegar, sugar, water, and salt to a simmer. Cook, stirring occasionally, until the sugar dissolves, about 1 minute. Transfer the liquid to a bowl and refrigerate until cooled, about 2 hours. (For a quick chill, you can put the liquid in the freezer for about 20 minutes.) The pickling liquid will keep, covered, in the refrigerator for a few days.

In a shallow bowl, combine the cucumber slices, chilled pickling liquid, jalapeño, and cilantro. The relish will keep, covered, in the refrigerator for 24 hours.

Cabbage Kimchi

 MAKES ABOUT 2 QUARTS

I used to think making your own kimchi was akin to making soap; why go through the process when you can buy it so inexpensively? Well, it turns out there's something very satisfying about the process. Plus, when you make it, you know exactly what's in it (occasionally kimchi contains a flour-water paste to thicken the juice). Cabbage kimchi is one of hundreds of types of Korean pickled vegetables collectively known as kimchi. Because the cabbage version is the most popular, it's often just referred to as "kimchi." Dr. Kim Song, my friend Howard's mom and a fantastic Korean home cook, was kind enough to teach me the method of kimchi making and share her personal recipe as well.

Although it takes a few days to reach the finished product, the effort involved is quite minimal. First the cabbage sits in salt brine for several hours to release excess liquid. Then you mix the drained cabbage with a spice paste and let it sit for a day or two to start the fermentation. At this point the cabbage is ready to refrigerate and serve as a side dish, or you can let it age—and ferment—for up to 1 month.

1/2 cup kosher salt

12 cups water

1 (3- to 3 1/2-pound) Napa cabbage, quartered lengthwise, then cut crosswise into 2-inch pieces

8 cloves garlic, minced

1/4 cup coarse Korean chili powder

3 tablespoons Asian fish sauce

1 tablespoon sugar

1 1/2 teaspoons minced fresh ginger

2 green onions, white and green parts, thinly sliced

1/4 pound daikon radish, peeled and cut into matchstick strips (about 1 cup)

In a large bowl, mix the salt with the water. Rinse the cabbage and add it to the bowl. If the cabbage leaves stick out of the water, put a piece of plastic wrap directly on the surface of the water and then top it with a plate to submerge the cabbage. Let the cabbage soak at room temperature for at least 6 hours or overnight.

In a small bowl, stir together the garlic, chili powder, fish sauce, sugar, and ginger. Refrigerate until ready to use. (If you plan to make kimchi repeatedly, you can whip up a large batch of the spice paste in a food processor. Use what you need and store the remainder in the refrigerator, covered, until you need it, up to 1 month.)

Drain the cabbage in a colander and then squeeze it to remove any excess liquid. Rinse out the bowl, dry it, and return the cabbage to the bowl. Add the green onions and radish and stir to combine. Add the spice paste and mix with a large spatula or your hands until well combined. Transfer the kimchi and any accumulated liquid to a large jar with a lid (you may

HEADS UP

The cabbage will need to soak
for at least 6 hours.
Kimchi should ferment for
about 48 hours before serving.

need 2 quart-size canning jars) or a plastic container with a locking lid. The lid is important here—kimchi has a strong odor.

Let the kimchi stand at room temperature for 48 hours (less if your kitchen is much hotter than room temperature) to start the fermentation process. (You should notice some liquid accumulating at the bottom of the jar within the first 24 hours.) Stir the kimchi and serve immediately as a side dish or, replace the lid and put it in the refrigerator, where it will keep for 3 to 4 weeks. After about 1 week, use in recipes that suggest "aged" kimchi.

Yakuza Cucumber and Avocado Salad

 SERVES 4

I first tasted a similar salad at one of my favorite Japanese restaurants, Yakuza Lounge in Portland, Oregon. The way the crisp cucumbers and creamy avocados interacted with the punchy dressing really caught my attention. Although you can make the dressing ahead, you should really assemble the dish just before serving to keep the flavors fresh and the avocados from discoloring. And please don't skip out on salting the cucumbers; it's an important step. It allows all the extra liquid to drain into the sink instead of diluting your salad.

2 English cucumbers, quartered lengthwise, seeded, and sliced crosswise into $1/2$-inch slices

1 tablespoon salt

3 tablespoons mirin

$2^1/4$ teaspoons unseasoned rice vinegar

$2^1/4$ teaspoons toasted sesame oil

1 teaspoon grated fresh ginger

2 ripe avocados, cut into 1-inch cubes

$1^1/2$ tablespoons toasted sesame seeds

$1/2$ teaspoon shichimi togarashi (see page 17), for serving (optional)

Set a colander over an empty bowl or the sink. Add the cucumbers and sprinkle with the salt. Rub the salt into the cucumbers with your fingers. Let the cucumbers stand until they shed much of their excess liquid, about 20 minutes. Pat the cucumbers dry with paper towels to remove any excess salt and liquid. You want the cucumbers to taste seasoned, but if they seem excessively salty, give them a quick rinse; just be sure to pat them dry afterward.

In a small bowl, whisk together the mirin, rice vinegar, sesame oil, and ginger. The dressing will keep, covered, in the refrigerator for up to 1 day.

Just before serving, transfer the cucumbers and avocados to a serving bowl. Stir the dressing well and pour it evenly over the salad. Toss the salad very gently and then sprinkle with the sesame seeds and *shichimi togarashi*.

Chilled Asparagus *with Sesame Dressing*

 SERVES 4 TO 6

The flavor of sesame pairs perfectly with fresh asparagus. Here I give it a double dose using both sesame oil and toasted sesame seeds. By chilling the asparagus you have a great do-ahead dish, but it's perfectly fine to toss the dressing with hot asparagus as well. For a fancier presentation, arrange whole steamed asparagus spears on a platter and pour the dressing over the top.

1 tablespoon soy sauce or tamari GF

1 tablespoon sugar

1 tablespoon unseasoned rice vinegar

1 tablespoon toasted sesame oil

1 tablespoon vegetable oil

1 teaspoon grated fresh ginger

1/2 teaspoon salt

1/4 teaspoon freshly ground black pepper

Pinch of red pepper flakes

11/2 pounds asparagus, ends trimmed, stalks cut diagonally into 1-inch pieces

2 teaspoons toasted sesame seeds

In a small bowl, whisk together the soy sauce, sugar, rice vinegar, sesame oil, vegetable oil, ginger, salt, black pepper, and red pepper flakes. Set aside. (The dressing can be made ahead and kept, covered, in the refrigerator for up to 1 day.)

In a large pot of boiling water, cook the asparagus until crisp-tender, about 2 minutes. Drain the asparagus in a colander and rinse it with cold water or submerge it in ice water to stop the cooking. Transfer the asparagus to a bowl and refrigerate it, covered, until ready to use, up to 1 day ahead. Toss the asparagus with the sesame dressing and the sesame seeds just before serving.

VARIATION If asparagus is not in season, green beans make a perfect match for the dressing. Boil the beans until crisp-tender, about 3 minutes, and then drain and toss them with the dressing. Serve hot, or chill the beans and dressing separately for later.

HEADS UP

You'll need to refrigerate the asparagus until chilled, about 3 hours.

Bok Choy *with Oyster Sauce*

 SERVES 4

Asian markets sell a dazzling assortment of mini heads of bok choy, choy sum, Shanghai bok choy, and the like. All of these types work well with the oyster sauce, or you can just cut regular bok choy into bite-size pieces. Blanching the vegetable first may seem excessive, but it makes it much easier to fit all the bok choy in the sauté pan at once. If you want to skip this step you may need to sauté the bok choy in batches.

1½ pounds baby bok choy, ends trimmed, leaves and stems cut into 1-inch pieces

3 tablespoons store-bought GF or homemade chicken broth (page 37)

1½ tablespoons oyster sauce GF

1 teaspoon soy sauce or tamari GF

¼ teaspoon salt

1 tablespoon vegetable oil

1 tablespoon shredded fresh ginger

Bring a large pot of water to a boil. Add the bok choy and cook for 1 minute (do this in two batches if necessary). Drain the bok choy in a colander and rinse it with cold water or submerge it in ice water to stop the cooking. Transfer the bok choy to paper towels or a clean dishtowel to remove excess water. Be sure to pat it dry or the sauce will be watery. The bok choy can be blanched earlier in the day and refrigerated until ready to use.

In a small bowl, stir together the chicken broth, oyster sauce, soy sauce, and salt. Set aside.

In a large frying pan or a wok, heat the oil over medium-high heat. Add the ginger and cook until sizzling and fragrant, about 1 minute. Add the bok choy and cook, stirring frequently, until crisp-tender, about 2 minutes. Stir in the sauce and cook until it coats the bok choy and everything is heated through, 1 to 2 minutes longer. Taste and add more salt if necessary. Serve hot.

VARIATIONS For stir-fried greens, trim the leaves only off one large head of regular bok choy and cut them into thin ribbons. Add them to the pan (without blanching) just after the ginger and stir-fry until wilted. Finish with the sauce as directed. Save the bok choy stems for another use. The greens will be enough for 2 servings.

Greens in Smoky Dashi Broth

 SERVES 4

When I tire of my standard go-to vegetable preparation (sautéed with garlic and oil), I turn to this simple yet impressive side dish. Blanch a mound of fresh spinach and chill it in a simple combination of dashi and soy sauce; the broth enhances other vegetables equally well, so don't be afraid to try your favorite. Instead of the chilled version you can serve the vegetables immediately while they're hot, but the flavor does improve as it marinates.

1 pound spinach, tough stems trimmed and discarded

1 cup dashi (page 36)

1¹/₂ tablespoons soy sauce or tamari GF

Toasted sesame seeds, for serving (optional)

Bonito flakes, for serving (optional)

HEADS UP

This dish calls for dashi (page 36). You can prepare it up to 4 days ahead.
If you decide to serve this dish cold, you'll need to refrigerate the vegetables in the marinade until chilled, for about 3 hours and up to 24 hours.

Bring a pot of water to a simmer. Add the spinach and cook until bright green and wilted, 1 to 2 minutes. Drain the spinach in a colander and then plunge it into a bowl of ice water to stop the cooking. When the spinach cools, put it on a clean kitchen towel, roll it up, and squeeze tightly to release any extra liquid.

In a serving bowl or a small platter with a rim, combine the dashi and the soy sauce. Add the spinach to the liquid and toss to combine. Serve immediately or refrigerate (my preference), covered, for up to 24 hours. Sprinkle with toasted sesame seeds and a touch of bonito flakes before serving.

VARIATIONS Experiment with your favorite green vegetable, or use a combination. Asparagus, green beans, and broccoli all work well, as do wedges of steamed winter squash, especially in combination with the spinach, broccoli rabe, or mustard greens.

Eggplant *with Sweet Miso Glaze*

 SERVES 4

Soaking the eggplant in salt water helps remove some of the vegetable's bitterness. I tried three different methods (the salt-water soak, sprinkling the eggplant pieces with salt in a colander, and no pre-salting) and preferred the salt water approach. The miso glaze tastes great on all kinds of vegetables. Brush it onto grilled corn-on-the-cob or onion wedges, stir it into a cherry tomato sauté, or try one of the roasted vegetable variations.

1¹/₂ pounds eggplant (1 large or 2 medium), peeled

3 tablespoons salt

4 cups warm water

1 tablespoon vegetable oil

¹/₂ cup Sweet Miso Glaze (page 28)

Toasted sesame seeds, for serving

2 green onions, white and green parts, thinly sliced, for serving

HEADS UP

This dish calls for Sweet Miso Glaze (page 28). You can prepare it up to 1 week ahead.

Cut the eggplant lengthwise into ³/₄-inch slices and then cut them in half crosswise. In a large bowl, dissolve the salt in the water. Add the eggplant to the salt water and top with a small plate to submerge it. Let the eggplant soak for about 20 minutes. Drain the eggplant in a colander and rinse with cold water. Transfer the eggplant to a clean kitchen towel or paper towels and blot it dry.

Preheat the broiler. Transfer the eggplant to an aluminum foil–lined baking sheet. Brush the eggplant with the oil. Broil the eggplant, about 4 inches from the heat source, until starting to soften, about 6 minutes. Remove the pan from the oven and brush the tops of the eggplant slices with some of the miso sauce. Flip the eggplant and brush the other side with the sauce. Return the pan to the oven and broil until golden and bubbly, about 4 minutes. Keep an eye on it to make sure the glaze doesn't burn. Serve the eggplant sprinkled with the sesame seeds and green onions.

VARIATION Use asparagus instead of eggplant. Toss the spears with some of the miso glaze on a baking sheet. Roast at 450°F until crisp-tender, 10 to 15 minutes. You can try the same method with green beans or halved brussels sprouts.

Tofu and Kimchi Stew

 SERVES 4 AS A MAIN DISH

When I used to frequent Korean restaurants, the jigae (stew) section of the menu always captivated me. The fiercely bubbling stews showed up at the table in individual iron cooking pots, certain to keep the stew hot throughout the meal if not all day. Kimchi and tofu remains one of the most popular combinations, though many types—including seafood versions—are available. As kimchi ages, it takes on more of a sour flavor, ideal for this particular dish. If you're using homemade kimchi, this is the time to use the old stuff. Be aware that different brands of kimchi and red chili powder can vary significantly in their levels of spiciness. Taste the broth a few times while it's cooking and make adjustments where needed, adding more chili powder—or fresh jalapeños—for more heat, or diluting the stew with a bit more liquid if you've gone too far.

1/2 pound thinly sliced pork belly or uncured bacon, cut crosswise into 1/4-inch-thick strips

2 tablespoons toasted sesame oil

8 cloves garlic, minced

2 teaspoons Korean chili powder, or substitute 2 teaspoons paprika mixed with 1/4 teaspoon cayenne pepper

3 cups kimchi GF, cut into bite-size pieces, plus 1/4 cup of the liquid

4 cups store-bought GF or home-made chicken broth (page 37)

1 pound firm tofu, cut into 1/2-inch cubes

4 green onions, white and green parts, coarsely chopped

1 to 2 tablespoons yellow miso paste GF

Steamed rice, for serving

··

HEADS UP

The pork needs to marinate for at least 15 minutes before making the soup.

In a small bowl, combine the pork with the sesame oil, garlic, and chili powder. Let stand at room temperature for at least 15 minutes, or in the refrigerator for up to several hours. Heat a pot over medium heat. Add the pork and its marinade and cook, stirring occasionally, until the pork is cooked through, about 5 minutes. Add the kimchi and its liquid and the chicken broth and bring to a boil. Lower the heat and simmer, partially covered, for 30 minutes.

Stir in the tofu and green onions. Simmer until the flavors are well combined, about 10 minutes longer. Turn off the heat and stir in 1 tablespoon of the miso until it dissolves. Taste the broth and, if it could use a little more saltiness, stir in the remaining 1 tablespoon miso. Serve the stew hot with steamed rice on the side.

VARIATIONS Add a dozen clams along with the tofu. Cover the pan and cook until the clams open, 5 to 10 minutes. Discard any clams that fail to open.

For a spicier version, add several slices of fresh jalapeño to the stew after stirring in the miso paste.

Try 1/2 pound sliced shiitake mushrooms instead of the pork for a meat-free version.

Add 2 ounces of soaked cellophane noodles to the broth with the tofu.

Braised Tofu in Mushroom Sauce

 SERVES 4

When the weather turns cool, my thoughts turn to stews and braised dishes. Unlike a big hunk of beef that takes hours to braise, tender cubes of tofu take on the flavor of the sauce in just minutes. You can find mushroom broth in the soup aisle of most grocery stores; check the label to choose a gluten-free brand. And if you like added kick, stir in a touch of chili-garlic sauce (Sriracha) at the table.

1/4 cup potato starch

21/2 tablespoons vegetable oil, divided

1 pound firm tofu, cut into 11/2 by 1/2-inch cubes, drained on paper towels for 15 minutes

Salt

Freshly ground black pepper

3 cloves garlic, minced

1 tablespoon minced fresh ginger

1/4 pound shiitake mushrooms, thinly sliced

1/4 pound green beans, cut into 1/2-inch lengths

1 tablespoon soy sauce or tamari **GF**

1 tablespoon sake or dry sherry

1/2 teaspoon sugar

1 cup mushroom broth **GF**

Red jalapeño chile, thinly sliced, for serving

Put the potato starch on a small plate. Heat 1 tablespoon of the oil in a large nonstick frying pan over medium-high heat. Season the tofu with salt and pepper and then dip the two larger sides of each tofu cube into the potato starch, tapping off any excess. (Discard the potato starch left on the plate.) Add the tofu to the pan and cook until light golden, 2 to 3 minutes per side. Transfer the tofu to a plate. Wipe out the pan.

In the same pan, heat the remaining 11/2 tablespoons oil over medium heat. Add the garlic and ginger and cook until fragrant, about 1 minute. Add the mushrooms and green beans and cook, stirring occasionally, until the mushrooms soften, about 3 minutes. Stir in the soy sauce, sake, and sugar. Add the mushroom broth and bring to a simmer.

Return the tofu cubes to the pan. Cover the pan and simmer gently, turning the tofu once, until heated through, 10 to 15 minutes. Sprinkle with jalapeño.

Winter Squash and Tofu Curry

 SERVES 4

Because winter squash pairs so well with warm spices like cinnamon and cumin, I wanted to make the curry with a blend of dried spices, Indian style. However, I also love Thai versions of pumpkin and tofu curry. Consider this a hybrid: a blend of Indian spices for background flavor plus—in the Thai spirit—a hit of crunchy peanuts, lime juice, and cilantro at the end.

2 tablespoons vegetable oil

1 small onion, chopped

3 cloves garlic, minced

1 tablespoon minced fresh ginger

³/₄ pound butternut or other winter squash, peeled and cut into ³/₄-inch dice (2 cups)

1 red bell pepper, cut into 1-inch pieces

2 teaspoons brown sugar

1 teaspoon turmeric

1 teaspoon ground cinnamon

³/₄ teaspoon ground coriander

³/₄ teaspoon ground cumin

¹/₄ teaspoon red pepper flakes

2 teaspoons salt

1 teaspoon Sriracha or other chili-garlic sauce **GF**

1 (14-ounce) can unsweetened coconut milk

¹/₂ cup water

12 ounces extra-firm tofu, cut into 1-inch cubes

2 tablespoons freshly squeezed lime juice

3 tablespoons chopped roasted peanuts

¹/₄ cup chopped fresh cilantro

Heat the oil in a large saucepan over medium heat. Add the onion and cook, stirring occasionally, until starting to soften, 3 to 4 minutes. Stir in the garlic, ginger, and squash. Cook over low heat, covered, for 5 minutes. Uncover the pan and add the red bell pepper, brown sugar, turmeric, cinnamon, coriander, cumin, red pepper flakes, and salt. Stir to combine. Cook, covered, until the squash starts to soften, about 5 minutes longer.

Add the Sriracha, coconut milk, and water to the pan and bring to a simmer. Gently stir in the tofu and simmer the curry, partially covered, until the squash is tender, about 15 minutes. Stir in the lime juice. Serve the curry hot, sprinkled with the peanuts and cilantro.

Chilled Tofu *with Cucumber Sunomono*

 SERVES 4

I conducted several experiments marinating chilled tofu, hoping to create a simple, yet intriguing result. Each time the overall dish seemed to be missing something, a problem solved by serving the tofu on a bed of lightly seasoned cucumber. Along with sesame seeds and green onion, I top the tofu with a generous pinch of bonito flakes. These dried, smoked fish flakes form the backbone of Japanese dashi broth (and consequently miso soup). Their addictive smoky quality adds a complex layer of flavor to the tofu and may become your new secret weapon.

1 pound soft tofu, cut into 1¹/₂-inch cubes

1 English cucumber, halved lengthwise, seeded, and thinly sliced crosswise

1 teaspoon salt

2 tablespoons unseasoned rice vinegar

1 tablespoon sugar

¹/₄ teaspoon red pepper flakes

3 teaspoons soy sauce or tamari **GF**, divided

1 tablespoon grated fresh ginger

1 tablespoon toasted sesame seeds, for serving

2 green onions, white and green parts, minced, for serving

Bonito flakes, for serving

HEADS UP

The cucumbers need to drain for 20 minutes and then marinate for at least 15 minutes before serving.

Put the tofu on a plate lined with paper towels or a clean kitchen towel to absorb excess liquid. Keep the tofu refrigerated until ready to use, changing the paper towels if they get too saturated with liquid.

Set a colander over an empty bowl or the sink. Transfer the cucumbers to the colander and sprinkle with the salt. Rub the salt into the cucumbers with your fingers. Let the cucumbers stand until they shed some of their excess liquid, about 20 minutes. Pat the cucumbers dry with paper towels to remove any excess salt and liquid.

In a bowl, mix together the rice vinegar, sugar, red pepper flakes, and 1 teaspoon of the soy sauce. Add the cucumbers and toss to combine. Transfer the cucumbers to the refrigerator to marinate for at least 15 minutes and up to several hours.

For serving, put the cucumber sunomono on a platter or a deep plate and top with the tofu. Pour the remaining 2 teaspoons soy sauce over the tofu cubes. Take the grated ginger in your hand and squeeze it over the tofu cubes, coating them with about 1¹/₂ teaspoons of juice (discard the pulp). Sprinkle with the sesame seeds, green onions, and bonito flakes.

VARIATIONS Try topping the tofu with shredded shiso leaves, daikon sprouts, toasted nori strips, sliced jalapeño chiles, or minced garlic.

Seafood

It always surprises me how many gifted home cooks shy away from cooking fish. A mysterious aura surrounds the process—as if only restaurant chefs can master seafood cooking. Not so, my friends! The most difficult part of cooking seafood at home is procuring a beautiful piece of fresh fish. Once you've tackled that, the cooking part is easy. Most fish cooks in less than 15 minutes. If you like fish, but rarely cook it, give it a try; you'll appreciate the addition to your repertoire.

Locating this show-stopping seafood may take no effort or a little bit of work, depending on where you live. In my area of the Pacific Northwest, I have many options for finding a wide variety of high-quality seafood. My favorite places to shop for fish are Asian markets, small independent fish markets, and Whole Foods. Many other grocery stores have lovely, well-kept fish counters. Fish steaks and fillets, shrimp, scallops, and calamari (squid) should look moist and vibrant. In the market they should be well chilled, preferably stored over ice. If you take a whiff, fish should smell a little briny, like the sea. Clams and mussels are purchased live; they should be living in a tank of moving water, or at least stored over ice. When you get home, unwrap clams and mussels and store them on top of a bowl of ice in the refrigerator, uncovered. I remove fish fillets and steaks from their packaging and put them on a paper towel–lined plate, covered with plastic wrap, in the refrigerator. Use the seafood within a day, two if it is absolutely fresh.

Perfect seafood needs little embellishment, but in this chapter I share a range of ideas and techniques for the gluten-free diner. Sautéed fish often gets dredged in flour before cooking; here, catfish gets a similar treatment only with seasoned rice flour. Because breadcrumbs don't make the cut, my crusted salmon gets a crisp coat of sesame seeds to keep things interesting. And instead of a heavy batter, tapioca flour dusts rings of calamari for a restaurant-worthy version of salt and pepper squid. Although the recipes specify a certain type of fish or shellfish, it is perfectly acceptable for you to substitute another fish with a similar flavor and texture, and with what is fresh and available.

Grilled Tuna Salad *with Ginger Carrot Dressing*

 SERVES 4

Try to find a mix of spicy greens for the salad, such as mizuna and watercress. If not, a mesclun mix works perfectly well, too, because you still have the radishes to add a peppery bite. Ideally, the tuna should be rare to medium-rare, but if that's not to your taste, cook it a bit longer than the recipe instructs. The salad makes a simple main dish, perfect for a hot summer night.

$1^{1}/_{2}$ pounds tuna steak, about 1 inch thick, cut into 4 pieces

1 teaspoon salt, divided

$^{1}/_{2}$ teaspoon freshly ground black pepper, divided

$4^{1}/_{2}$ tablespoons soy sauce or tamari GF, divided

3 tablespoons chopped fresh ginger

3 green onions, white and green parts, coarsely chopped

1 large carrot, peeled and cut into chunks

$^{1}/_{4}$ cup freshly squeezed lemon juice

$1^{1}/_{2}$ tablespoons toasted sesame oil

$1^{1}/_{2}$ tablespoons water

$^{1}/_{3}$ cup plus 1 tablespoon vegetable oil, divided

8 ounces mixed greens (about 14 cups loosely packed)

1 bunch radishes, thinly sliced

1 tablespoon toasted sesame seeds

On a plate, combine the tuna with $^{3}/_{4}$ teaspoon of the salt, $^{1}/_{4}$ teaspoon of the pepper, and $1^{1}/_{2}$ tablespoons of the soy sauce. Set aside while you make the dressing. Or refrigerate it, covered, for up to 2 hours.

Combine the ginger, green onions, and carrot in the bowl of a food processor. Pulse several times to chop the ingredients. Scrape down the bowl with a spatula and then add the lemon juice, sesame oil, water, and the remaining 3 tablespoons soy sauce, $^{1}/_{4}$ teaspoon salt, and $^{1}/_{4}$ teaspoon pepper. Turn the food processor on and with the motor running, add $^{1}/_{3}$ cup of the vegetable oil in a steady stream through the feed tube. The dressing can be kept, covered, in the refrigerator for up to 1 day.

Preheat the grill to medium-high. Coat the tuna with the remaining 1 tablespoon vegetable oil. Oil the grill rack to keep the fish from sticking. Cook the tuna for 3 minutes. Flip and cook until done to your taste, about 3 minutes longer for medium-rare. Transfer the tuna to a cutting board.

In a large bowl, toss the greens and the radishes with half the dressing. Transfer the salad to 4 plates. Top each salad with a piece of tuna. Spoon some of the remaining dressing over the tuna and greens, or pass it at the table. Sprinkle with the sesame seeds.

VARIATIONS Instead of grilling, sear the tuna in a pan over medium-high heat.

Salmon is a good substitute for the tuna, as is pork tenderloin.

Steamed Sea Bass *with Sizzling Ginger*

 SERVES 4

If you consider yourself one of the many skittish fish cooks out there, try this technique for sautéed-then-steamed sea bass. All you need is a super-hot nonstick pan and a touch of oil. After a brief sear on one side, flip the fish, add the seasonings to the pan, and cover it with a tight-fitting lid. Finish the cooking by steaming the fish gently off the flame, keeping it moist and perfect. Sea bass has a rather high (healthy) oil content that isn't to everyone's liking, but you can use another medium-firm to firm-textured fish if you prefer.

---

1 tablespoon plus 2 teaspoons vegetable oil, divided

1¹/₂ tablespoons minced fresh ginger

6 green onions, white and green parts, thinly sliced

1 red jalapeño chile, minced

1¹/₂ pounds sea bass fillets, about 1 inch thick, skin removed, cut into 4 pieces

¹/₂ teaspoon salt

¹/₄ teaspoon freshly ground black pepper

1 tablespoon soy sauce or tamari **GF**

2 tablespoons sake

Steamed rice, for serving (optional)

In a large nonstick frying pan, heat 1 tablespoon of the oil over medium heat. Add the ginger, green onions, and jalapeño and cook until sizzling and fragrant, 1 to 2 minutes. Transfer to a small bowl.

Pat the fish very dry with paper towels. Heat the remaining 2 teaspoons oil in the same pan over medium-high heat until very hot, about 3 minutes. Sprinkle the fish with salt and pepper. Cook the fish until golden brown, about 2 minutes. Flip the fish with a spatula. Evenly spoon the green onion mixture over the fish. Have the lid to the pan in hand as you pour the soy sauce and sake into the pan. (Pour the liquid into the pan, not onto the fish.) Immediately cover the pan with the lid and remove the pan from the heat. Let the fish steam until cooked through, about 10 minutes for 1-inch-thick fillets. (Adjust the cooking time according to the thickness of the fish, about 8 minutes for ³/₄-inch fillets and up to 14 minutes for 1¹/₂-inch fillets.) Serve the fish hot with the pan juices spooned over the top.

VARIATIONS Instead of sea bass, try cod, rockfish, halibut, salmon, or your favorite medium-firm to firm-textured fish. Sear for 2 minutes and then adjust the steaming time according to size.

Sautéed Catfish *with Peanuts and Fresh Herbs*

 SERVES 4

Since my early memories of catfish bring to mind cornmeal-crusted mud, I wanted to give this underrated fish another chance to win me over. I treated it to a very special Vietnamese-inspired preparation: a light sauté of rice flour-and-turmeric dusted catfish followed by a shower of fresh wilted herbs—delicious! The majority of catfish available today is farm raised, eliminating much of the murky flavor of its wild cousins. And while I'm generally not a huge fan of farmed fish, I actually prefer sustainably raised farmed catfish from the United States. Serve the fish over a bed of cooked rice vermicelli for a one-dish meal.

1½ pounds catfish fillets, about ¼ inch thick, skin removed, cut into 1½-inch pieces

½ cup rice flour

2 teaspoons salt

1½ teaspoons turmeric

½ teaspoon freshly ground black pepper

3 tablespoons vegetable oil, divided, plus more if needed

6 green onions, white and green parts, thinly sliced

¼ cup unsalted peanuts

½ cup chopped fresh dill

1 cup packed fresh cilantro leaves

Cooked rice vermicelli, for serving (optional)

Nuoc cham (page 27), for serving

HEADS UP
The dish calls for *nuoc cham* (page 27). You can prepare it up to 2 weeks ahead.

If the catfish feels wet or if it was previously frozen, pat it dry with paper towels or a clean kitchen towel. Combine the rice flour, salt, turmeric, and pepper in a gallon-size resealable bag or on a wide, rimmed plate. Add half the fish and shake to coat with the seasoned flour. Heat 1 tablespoon of the oil in a large nonstick frying pan over medium-high heat. Remove the fish from the bag, shaking any excess flour back into the bag. Add the seasoned catfish to the pan and cook until golden and cooked through, 2 to 3 minutes per side for ¼-inch-thick fillets. Transfer the fish to a platter or large plate. Repeat with the remaining fish and 1 tablespoon more oil.

When all the fish is cooked, wipe the pan clean. Heat the remaining 1 tablespoon oil over medium heat. Add the green onions and peanuts and cook, stirring, until sizzling and fragrant, about 1 minute. Stir in the dill and cilantro and cook until wilted, about 1 minute. Pour the fresh herb mixture over the catfish. Serve over rice vermicelli with *nuoc cham* on the side for drizzling.

VARIATION I used farm-raised catfish fillets, but you could try another medium-firm textured fillet, such as striped bass or flounder. The catfish I use is fairly thin (about ¼ inch thick); add a few minutes to the cooking time if you use thicker fillets.

Black Cod Broiled *with Savory Miso Glaze*

 SERVES 4

You need to plan ahead to give the fish time to marinate, but otherwise this dinner party–worthy dish couldn't be simpler. Once you make the marinade and brush it on the fish, you can forget about the whole thing for a day or so until it's time to hit the broiler. The pickled ginger adds a perfect spark of acidity to the fish that I find essential; please give it a try.

1¹/₂ **pounds black cod fillets, about 1 inch thick, cut into 4 pieces**

³/₄ **cup savory miso glaze (page 29)**

Store-bought GF or homemade pickled ginger (page 35), for serving

HEADS UP

You'll need to marinate the fish for at least 8 and up to 24 hours.
This dish calls for Savory Miso Glaze (page 29). You can prepare it up to 2 weeks ahead.
If you choose to make your own pickled ginger (page 35), you can prepare it 1 day ahead.

Transfer the fish to a gallon-size resealable bag or glass baking dish. If you've just made the miso glaze, make sure it is completely cooled. (Transfer to the freezer for 20 minutes to cool it quickly.) Pour the miso glaze over the fish. Let the fish marinate, refrigerated, for at least 8 hours and preferably 24 hours, turning the bag occasionally to ensure the marinade completely coats the fish. The flavor will increase the longer it marinates.

Heat the broiler. Line a broiler pan with aluminum foil. Wipe any excess marinade from the fish and transfer the fillets to the broiler pan. Broil the fish, about 4 inches from the heat, until golden brown, about 7 minutes. Turn off the broiler and continue cooking the fish in the hot oven until cooked through, about 5 minutes longer for 1-inch-thick fillets. Serve hot with pickled ginger slices.

VARIATION Substitute salmon, true cod, or Spanish mackerel for the black cod, adding from 2 to 4 minutes for thicker cuts. You can also grill the fish instead of broiling it. Because there's sugar in the marinade, keep the heat moderate to avoid burning the fish and flip it once during grilling.

Sesame-Crusted Salmon

 SERVES 4

Sometimes I miss the crunch of a breadcrumb coating, so I wanted to create that same effect without the gluten. Coating the salmon with a layer of sesame seeds, held in place by a cornstarch and egg white "glue," forms a crust that is super crisp and exactly what I imagined. Just keep an eye on the heat; you want it high enough to brown the seeds without burning them.

1¹/₂ pounds salmon fillets, about 1¹/₂ inches thick, cut into 4 pieces

Salt and freshly ground black pepper

1 egg white

2 tablespoons cornstarch

¹/₂ cup sesame seeds

2 tablespoons vegetable oil

About ¹/₂ cup store-bought **GF**, or homemade Teriyaki Sauce (page 26), more if needed

HEADS UP
This dish calls for teriyaki sauce (page 26). If you choose to make your own, you can prepare it up to 2 weeks ahead.

Season the salmon with salt and pepper. In a small bowl, whisk together the egg white and the cornstarch until well combined. (This will be a bit messy at first, but it will come together.) Pour the sesame seeds onto a plate. Brush the skinless side of the salmon fillets with the egg white mixture and then dip them into the sesame seeds to coat.

In a large frying pan, heat the oil over medium-high heat. Put the salmon in the pan, sesame-seed side down. Lower the heat to medium. Cook until the crust is golden, about 5 minutes, checking a little earlier to make sure it's not browning too quickly (if it is, flip the fish). Flip the salmon; continue cooking until cooked through, about 5 minutes longer for 1¹/₂-inch-thick fillets.

As the salmon finishes cooking, baste the tops and sides with the teriyaki sauce, or to maintain the crisp crust, serve the salmon with the warm sauce poured around it. (If you made the sauce ahead of time, reheat it briefly in a small saucepan or in the microwave.)

VARIATIONS Substitute 1¹/₂ pounds large sea scallops for the salmon. Coat each of the two flat sides with the egg white mixture and the sesame seeds and then proceed with the recipe. Cook the scallops for 3 minutes per side. You can coat slabs of firm tofu the same way. Drain the tofu for a few minutes on paper towels before brushing it with the egg white mixture.

Rice Paper–Wrapped Salmon
in Green Curry Sauce

 SERVES 4

While playing around in the kitchen one day, I decided to roll a piece of fish in rice paper before cooking it to see what would happen. The rice paper browned and crisped in the sauté pan beautifully, which inspired this recipe—one that can be served even for special occasions. You will have enough leftover curry paste to make Green Curry Chicken (page 153) or you can freeze the paste for later. Try the recipe with halibut as well.

1 (14-ounce) can unsweetened coconut milk

8 tablespoons Fresh Green Curry Paste (page 33), divided

1 tablespoon brown sugar

1 tablespoon Asian fish sauce

$1/2$ teaspoon salt

Grated zest of 1 lime, plus lime wedges for serving

$1^1/2$ pounds salmon fillets, about 1 inch thick, skin removed, cut into 4 pieces

4 (8 to 9-inch) rice paper wrappers (also called spring roll wrappers or spring roll skins), made from rice or tapioca flour

1 tablespoon vegetable oil

$1/3$ cup chopped fresh cilantro

Jasmine rice, for serving (optional)

HEADS UP

The dish calls for Fresh Green Curry Paste (page 33). You can prepare it up to 3 days ahead.

To make the sauce, spoon the layer of thick coconut milk from the top of the can and put it in a small saucepan, reserving the remaining liquid. Bring to a simmer and then whisk in 6 tablespoons of the curry paste. Simmer gently for 5 minutes. Stir in the brown sugar, fish sauce, salt, lime zest, and the remaining coconut milk. Simmer until thickened, about 10 minutes.

Sprinkle a pinch of salt over each salmon fillet. Spread the remaining 2 tablespoons curry paste over the top of the fillets. Fill a large bowl with warm water. Soak 2 of the rice paper wrappers in the water until pliable, about 30 seconds. Carefully remove the wrappers from the water and set them on a clean kitchen towel. Arrange a piece of the fish on top of each wrapper. Lift the lower part of the wrapper up over the fish; fold in the sides, and then fold down the top to enclose the fish in rice paper. Transfer the wrapped salmon to a plate and repeat with the remaining fish.

Heat the oil in a large nonstick frying pan over medium-high heat. Add the wrapped fish to the pan, seam-sides down, and cook until golden, about 2 minutes. Flip the fish and cook until golden, 2 to 3 minutes longer for 1-inch-thick fillets. Add a few more minutes for thicker fish. Reheat the sauce if needed, stirring in the cilantro just before serving. Serve the fish hot with the curry sauce and jasmine rice. Pass the lime wedges at the table.

Salt and Pepper Squid

 SERVES 6 AS AN APPETIZER

Don't go dusting off an ancient jar of ground black pepper for this recipe; its simplicity relies on freshly ground pepper. After you procure some fragrant peppercorns (I used Telicherry), grind them in a clean coffee grinder or a pepper mill set to a coarse setting. If you lack either of these resources, put the peppercorns in a plastic bag and smash them with a mallet—freshly ground pepper and aggression management! Fried squid is often coated with a wheat flour–based batter, but I experimented with several versions of the squid using tapioca, rice flour, or cornstarch as a coating. You could use any of the three, but I found the tapioca flour maintained the crispest crust as the squid cooled. Use a deep-fry thermometer to accurately gauge the oil temperature.

Vegetable oil for frying

1¹/₂ pounds squid (calamari), bodies cut into thin rings, tentacles halved if large

1¹/₂ tablespoons kosher salt

1 tablespoon coarsely ground black peppercorns

³/₄ cup tapioca flour (also called tapioca starch)

Lime wedges, for serving

Fiery Ginger Sauce (page 30) or Super Secret Spicy Sauce (page 32), for serving (optional)

HEADS UP

This dish calls for either the Fiery Ginger Sauce (page 30) or Super Secret Spicy Sauce (page 32). The latter can be made up to 3 days ahead and the former up to 2 weeks.

In a wok or a medium saucepan, heat about 3 inches of oil over medium heat to 375°F. This may take about 15 minutes. If you don't have a deep-fry thermometer, sprinkle a bit of tapioca flour in the oil; when it sizzles vigorously, it's ready. The oil should not get hot enough to smoke. While the oil is heating, pat the squid dry with paper towels. Excess moisture will cause the coating to clump and the oil to spatter.

Line a plate with paper towels. In a gallon-size resealable bag, combine the salt, pepper, and tapioca flour. Shake to combine. Add the squid to the bag and shake to coat. Take about one-third of the squid in your hand and shake any excess coating back into the bag. Carefully add the squid to the oil. Cook, stirring occasionally to keep the pieces from sticking together, until the squid is tender and starting to brown, 2 to 3 minutes. Remove the squid from the oil with a slotted spoon and transfer to the prepared plate. Repeat the process twice more with the remaining squid. Be sure to let the oil return to 375°F between batches. Serve each batch as it is cooked or keep warm in a low oven. Serve with lime wedges and one of the dipping sauces.

VARIATION Use medium peeled raw shrimp instead of squid; cook for about 3 minutes per batch.

Thai Seafood Salad

 SERVES 6 AS AN APPETIZER

Multiple types of shellfish combine to form a beautiful and tangy salad, perfect for a light summer lunch. Except for the mussels, the remaining seafood benefits from very brief and gentle poaching—it should spend just a few minutes in the pan at barely a simmer. Using an assortment of shellfish gives the salad a wide range of tastes and textures, but you can vary the mix. Substitute clams for the mussels or even add a bit of crab.

---

1 pound mussels

1/2 pound medium raw shrimp, peeled and deveined

1/2 pound bay scallops

1/2 pound calamari, cut into thin rings

3/4 cup halved cherry tomatoes

1/3 cup thinly sliced red onion

1/2 cup diced pineapple

1 jalapeño chile, thinly sliced

1/4 cup freshly squeezed lime juice

3 tablespoons Asian fish sauce

1/2 cup roughly chopped fresh cilantro

Put the mussels in a bowl of cold water and swish them around with your hands to remove any debris. Pick up the mussels one by one and debeard them by tugging back and forth on the bundle of hairy-looking black fibers emerging from the mussel. It should come out fairly easily.

Set a colander over a large bowl. In a medium saucepan, bring 1 cup of water to a boil over medium-high heat. Add the mussels and cover the pan. Cook for 3 minutes, shaking the pan occasionally. Remove the lid and check for open mussels. If all the mussels are still closed, replace the lid. As the mussels open, immediately remove them from the pan with a slotted spoon and transfer them to the colander. Discard any mussels that do not open after about 10 minutes.

When all the mussels are out of the pan, add the shrimp to the cooking liquid and lower the heat to medium-low (the liquid should be barely simmering, if at all). Cook the shrimp until pink and just cooked through, about 2 minutes. Remove the shrimp with a slotted spoon and add them to the colander. Add the scallops to the cooking liquid and cook until just done, about 2 minutes. Transfer the scallops to the colander. Add the calamari to the liquid and cook until the calamari just turns opaque, about 1 minute. Transfer the calamari to the colander.

Once the seafood has drained, discard any liquid that has collected in the bowl and then pour the seafood into the empty bowl. Add the cherry tomatoes, red onion, pineapple,

(continued)

(continued from page 140)

and jalapeño. Add the lime juice and fish sauce and toss gently to combine. Top with the cilantro leaves. Serve immediately or refrigerate for up to 2 hours. Do not refrigerate the mixed salad too long or the acidity in the lime juice will toughen the shellfish. If you prefer, refrigerate the cooked shellfish separately for several hours and toss it with the remaining ingredients closer to serving time.

VARIATIONS You don't need to use all of the shellfish suggested above, but use a minimum of two different types for the salad. For example, combine 1 pound of mussels or clams and 1^1/$_2$ pounds total of shrimp, scallops, crab, or calamari mix. Clams cook the same way as mussels; crabmeat is already cooked so you can toss it straight into the salad.

Miso Broth *with Steamed Clams*

Turn ubiquitous miso soup into a unique starter with the addition of steamed clams and cellophane noodles. To keep the noodles from tangling in the shells, I pull the steamed clam meat from the shells and toss it back into the soup. If you prefer the look of the whole clams, then leave them be, but prepare for a slightly more hands-on dining experience. Red miso offers a rich, full-bodied salinity to the dish, but you can substitute another variety if you have it on hand.

2 ounces dried cellophane (mung bean) noodles (sometimes called bean threads or sai fun)

2 pounds littleneck clams

3 cups dashi (page 36)

¹/₄ cup sake

4 green onions, white and green parts, minced

1 jalapeño chile, thinly sliced

3 tablespoons miso paste, preferably red **GF**

HEADS UP

This dish calls for dashi (page 36). You can prepare it up to 4 days ahead.

Soak the noodles in a bowl of hot tap water until softened, about 15 minutes. (If you can stretch out a noodle and it bounces back, it's done.) Drain the noodles in a colander and then cut them into smaller lengths with scissors.

While the noodles are soaking, put the clams in a bowl of cold water and swish them around with your hand to remove any dirt or grit. Pour off the water and repeat until the water stays clear, about three or four times. Drain the clams in a colander.

In a large pot, bring the dashi, sake, green onions, and jalapeño to a boil over medium-high heat. Add the clams and cover the pot with a lid. Cook for about 3 minutes, shaking the pot occasionally. Remove the lid and check for open clams. If all the clams are still closed, replace the lid. Keep checking the pot and as the clams open, immediately remove them with a slotted spoon and transfer them to a bowl. Discard any clams that do not open after about 10 minutes.

Lower the heat to medium-low and whisk the miso paste into the broth. Add the noodles and simmer very gently until cooked through, about 3 minutes. While the noodles simmer, remove the clam meat from the shells with a fork and add it to the soup. Serve hot.

NINE Poultry

Most families I know eat a lot of chicken, especially during the week. Because it cooks quickly and adapts well to many flavor combinations, chicken makes a perfect busy weeknight staple. Many of these recipes can also be made in advance and reheated, perfect for those who like to cook ahead. To help perfect your chicken-cooking skills, I've included some favorites that employ a number of different cooking methods, including stir-frying, poaching, braising, and even deep-frying. The most basic thing to remember about cooking chicken, especially white meat, is not to overcook it.

Personally, I prefer dark meat not only for its richer flavor, but also because it's much more forgiving. I offer plenty of options for both types (and a fantastic salad using minced duck, too), but if you do substitute white meat for dark be sure to cut back on the cooking time. The recipes always list general cooking times, but the size of chicken breasts can vary wildly. If you cook them on the bone, use a knife to check where the meat and bone meet, it should look moist and white, and just barely past pink.

In creating a collection of Asian chicken dishes, I focus on using alternative thickeners and tinkered with sauce ingredients to make old favorites gluten free. The ginger sauce that accompanies *Khao Man Gai* is normally made from wheat-based yellow soybean sauce. My miso-based version tastes just as great as the original. Japanese curries generally rely on a roux (actually called "curry roux") for thickening the sauce, but I found a touch of cornstarch and some good old-fashioned simmering did the trick. The Japanese Pub Fried Chicken, cloaked in a light cornstarch batter, tastes so good it makes the deep-frying totally worth it. As you work your way through the chapter, I hope you find several new favorite applications for that reliable old standby.

Minced Duck Salad *with Lime Dressing*

SERVES 4 AS AN APPETIZER

The origin of minced meat salads, known as larb *or* larp, *can be traced to the vibrant cuisine of Laos. Also popular in the Thai region of Isaan, the salad combines minced meat, shallots, and fresh herbs with a tart dressing of just lime juice and fish sauce—not even a trace of oil to weigh it down. I love the richness duck breast brings to the salad, but it can be expensive; you can try one of the many variations instead (boneless chicken thighs are my next favorite). Traditionally, toasted rice powder is incorporated into the salad to bind the juices and add a bit of texture. I prefer it without the rice powder, but see the variation below if you want to try it. Serve the salad wrapped in lettuce, over shredded cabbage leaves, or with sticky rice for more of a meal.*

1/2 cup water

Salt

1 pound boneless, skinless duck breast, cut into 1-inch slices

2 shallots, thinly sliced

1/4 cup freshly squeezed lime juice

3 tablespoons Asian fish sauce

1 red jalapeño chile, thinly sliced

3 green onions, white and green parts, thinly sliced

1/3 cup chopped fresh cilantro

1/3 cup chopped fresh mint

Cucumber slices, for serving

Lettuce or cabbage leaves, for serving

Sticky rice (page 101), optional

....

HEADS UP

If you're serving sticky rice with the salad, it needs to soak for several hours before cooking.

Bring the water and a large pinch of salt to a simmer in a medium saucepan. Add the duck to the water and simmer gently, stirring occasionally, until cooked through, about 8 minutes. Turn off the heat, remove the duck from the water with a slotted spoon, and transfer it to a cutting board. Add the sliced shallots to the pan and let them soften in the hot water for a few minutes. Using a knife, mince the duck; transfer the duck to a bowl.

Toss the duck with the lime juice and fish sauce. Remove the shallots from the pan with a slotted spoon and add them to the duck. Add the chile, green onions, cilantro, and mint and toss to combine. Serve the salad with cucumber slices on a bed of lettuce leaves or shredded cabbage. You an also serve the duck wrapped in lettuce leaves with cucumber matchsticks. Sticky rice makes a delicious and traditional accompaniment. The salad can be refrigerated, covered, for up to 4 hours. Add the lettuce or cabbage just before serving.

VARIATIONS Instead of duck, try chicken (I use boneless thighs), beef, pork, fish (a firm, white fish), or even turkey. You can start with ground meat or simmer larger pieces and then mince after cooking. You may need to adjust the cooking time slightly. Crab makes a wonderful salad as well; use cooked lump crabmeat and eliminate the

(continued)

(continued from page 147)

cooking step. Add the shallots raw or soak them in hot water for a few minutes to soften them.

Add halved cherry tomatoes or blanched green beans to the salad. Taste and add more lime juice or fish sauce if needed.

To make toasted rice powder, a traditional part of this recipe, heat a few tablespoons of raw jasmine rice in a small frying pan over low heat, stirring frequently, until the rice is light brown. Crush the rice to a powder in a clean spice grinder. Sprinkle about 1 tablespoon of rice powder over the salad.

Shredded Chicken *with Creamy Sesame Sauce*

 SERVES 4

You may recognize this Chinese dish as a version of Bon Bon (or Bang Bang) Chicken, *the common denominator being a creamy and spicy sesame sauce cloaking shredded ribbons of poached chicken. Here the chicken rests on a bed of cucumber strips, salted to remove excess liquid, but you could also toss the chicken and sauce with cooked rice noodles for an equally tasty meal. In fact, I use the sauce on lots of things—pork chops, grilled fish, broccoli, even rice with lentils. The sauce and chicken can both be made 1 day ahead and refrigerated until ready to use, but prepare the cucumbers just before serving.*

---

2 English cucumbers, peeled, halved lengthwise, seeded, and cut crosswise into thin slices

2 teaspoons salt

1 cup plus 3 tablespoons store-bought GF or homemade chicken broth (page 37)

1¹/₂ pounds boneless, skinless chicken breasts

Set a colander over an empty bowl or the sink. Add the cucumbers and sprinkle with the salt. Rub the salt into the cucumbers with your fingers. Let the cucumbers stand until they shed some of their excess liquid, about 20 minutes. Squeeze the cucumbers to release the last of the liquid and then pat them dry with paper towels or a clean kitchen towel to remove any remaining salt.

In a medium saucepan, bring 1 cup of the chicken broth to a simmer. Add the chicken and simmer gently for 8 minutes. Turn the chicken over with tongs and bring it just back to a simmer. Turn off the heat and let the chicken steam, covered, for 5 minutes. Remove the lid and quickly turn the chicken pieces over with tongs. Cover the pan and continue

3 cloves garlic, minced

1 tablespoon minced fresh ginger

2^1/$_2$ tablespoons soy sauce or tamari `GF`

2 tablespoons sesame tahini, well stirred

1 tablespoon toasted sesame oil

1 tablespoon vegetable oil

2 teaspoons sugar

^{1}/$_4$ teaspoon red pepper flakes

^{1}/$_4$ teaspoon freshly ground black pepper

^{1}/$_3$ cup chopped fresh cilantro

steaming until the chicken is cooked through, 5 to 10 minutes longer depending on the thickness of the chicken. Remove the chicken from the saucepan and, when cool enough to handle, pull it into shreds using two forks or your fingers. The chicken will keep, covered, in the refrigerator for up to 2 days.

While the chicken is cooking, make the sauce. In a blender, combine the remaining 3 tablespoons chicken broth, garlic, ginger, soy sauce, tahini, sesame oil, vegetable oil, sugar, red pepper flakes, and black pepper. Puree until smooth, about 1 minute. The sauce will keep, covered, in the refrigerator for up to 2 days. Bring it to room temperature before using.

For serving, arrange the drained cucumbers on a serving platter. Top the cucumbers with the shredded chicken and then the sauce. Sprinkle with the cilantro.

Kung Pao Chicken

 SERVES 4

Traditionally, the heat in this crowd-pleasing combo of diced chicken and peanuts aims to numb your tongue and bring sweat to your brow. Because the dish otherwise proves so family friendly, I cut the heat considerably. For a more authentic touch, you can add halved dried chiles, toss in some Szechuan peppercorns, or just increase the amount of red pepper flakes. Have all the components lined up and ready to go before you start cooking. Once you turn on the wok, things move fast.

1¹/₂ pounds boneless, skinless chicken breasts, cut into ¹/₂-inch dice

4 tablespoons soy sauce or tamari **GF**, divided

1 tablespoon sake or dry sherry

¹/₂ teaspoon salt

¹/₂ teaspoon freshly ground black pepper

2 tablespoons warm water

1 tablespoon sugar

2¹/₂ tablespoons unseasoned rice vinegar

2¹/₂ teaspoons toasted sesame oil

3 tablespoons vegetable oil, divided

1 tablespoon cornstarch

1 tablespoon minced fresh ginger

8 cloves garlic, minced

6 green onions, white and green parts, sliced

¹/₂ teaspoon red pepper flakes

¹/₂ cup coarsely chopped roasted peanuts or cashews

Steamed rice, for serving (optional)

In a medium bowl, stir together the chicken, 1 tablespoon of the soy sauce, the sake, salt, and pepper. Set aside until ready to use.

In a small bowl, stir together the warm water and sugar until the sugar dissolves. Add the rice vinegar, sesame oil, and the remaining 3 tablespoons soy sauce.

In a large frying pan or a wok, heat 1 tablespoon of the vegetable oil over medium-high heat. Add half the chicken to the pan and cook, stirring occasionally, until lightly browned but not all the way cooked through, about 2 minutes. Transfer the chicken to a large bowl. Repeat with the remaining chicken and 1 tablespoon of the oil. Add the cornstarch to the chicken. Toss to combine. Heat the remaining 1 tablespoon oil over medium-high heat. Add the ginger, garlic, green onions, and red pepper flakes and cook, stirring, for 1 minute. Add the chicken back to the pan and stir to coat. Stir in the soy sauce mixture and bring to a simmer. Cook until the sauce coats the chicken and everything is heated through, about 2 minutes longer. Stir in the peanuts; serve hot with steamed rice.

VARIATIONS You can add about 1 cup diced asparagus or 1 diced red bell pepper along with the green onions. Cook for 1 to 2 minutes longer.

Thai Coconut Chicken Soup

 SERVES 6 AS AN APPETIZER

The traditional version of tom kha gai *includes fragrant and aromatic lemongrass, galangal, and kaffir lime leaves to flavor the broth. The lemongrass and galangal are woody and fibrous; smash them with the side of your knife before cooking to release their flavors more quickly. I've seen plastic containers of both lemongrass and lime leaves in grocery stores near the fresh herbs. If you have trouble finding them, try one of the substitutions: while less authentic, the soup will still taste delicious and flavorful. (If possible, though, try to limit the number of substitutions to one.) Also, avoid potential chewing disasters by warning diners to scoot these woody ingredients to the side of the bowl; they're not edible. For more of a meal, serve with jasmine rice or stir in some cooked rice noodles.*

1 pound boneless skinless chicken breasts, cut into 1-inch cubes

2 tablespoons brown sugar

1/4 cup Asian fish sauce

3 cups store-bought GF or home-made chicken broth (page 37)

2 stalks lemongrass, bottom 4 inches only, smashed (or substitute the zest of 1 lemon, preferably in long strips)

1 (4-inch) piece fresh galangal (or substitute fresh ginger), cut diagonally into 6 slices and smashed

3 pairs kaffir lime leaves (or substitute the zest of 1 lime, preferably in long strips)

3 cups unsweetened coconut milk

6 ounces mushrooms, quartered

1/4 cup freshly squeezed lime juice

2 red jalapeño chiles, thinly sliced

1/4 cup chopped fresh cilantro

Steamed jasmine rice, for serving (optional)

In a medium bowl, combine the chicken with the brown sugar and fish sauce. Set aside.

In a large saucepan, bring the chicken broth, lemongrass, galangal, and lime leaves to a boil. Lower the heat and simmer for about 10 minutes. Add the coconut milk and mushrooms and bring the soup back to a boil.

Stir in the chicken and its marinade and simmer gently until the chicken is cooked through, about 5 minutes. Remove the pan from the heat and stir in the lime juice, jalapeños, and cilantro. Serve with jasmine rice on the side.

Green Curry Chicken

 SERVES 4

Before you try the version using store-bought curry paste, please promise you will try it at least once with the homemade Fresh Green Curry Paste (page 33). Don't let it scare you; it actually comes together in just a few minutes in the food processor, and will last up to a month in the freezer. The flavor difference is incomparable and I know you'll be very proud of your results. Once you have the curry paste ready to go, it's a downhill race. Lime leaves are often available near the fresh herbs in upscale groceries, or just substitute lime zest.

---

1 pound boneless, skinless chicken breasts

3 tablespoons Asian fish sauce

1 (14-ounce) can unsweetened coconut milk

1/2 cup Fresh Green Curry Paste (page 33) or 3 tablespoons store-bought green curry paste GF

1 cup store-bought GF or home-made chicken broth (page 37)

2 pairs kaffir lime leaves, or substitute the zest of 1 lime, preferably in long strips

1 Japanese eggplant (about 6 ounces), quartered lengthwise, and then cut crosswise into 1-inch pieces

1/2 cup drained and rinsed canned bamboo shoots

1/3 cup chopped fresh basil, Thai basil, or cilantro

Steamed jasmine rice, for serving

Cut the chicken crosswise into thin slices. Stack the slices and cut the meat into thin strips. Combine the chicken and the fish sauce in a bowl. Set aside until ready to use.

Spoon the layer of thick coconut milk from the top of the can and into a saucepan, setting aside the remaining liquid. Bring to a simmer and then whisk in the curry paste. Simmer gently for 5 minutes. Stir in the remaining coconut milk, the chicken broth, lime leaves, and eggplant. Bring to a boil; lower the heat and simmer for 10 minutes.

Stir in the chicken and the bamboo shoots and simmer until the chicken is cooked through, about 5 minutes. Remove the pan from the heat and stir in the basil. (If you used purchased curry paste, you may need to add a little salt. Taste the curry and add about 1/4 to 1/2 teaspoon of salt if needed.) Serve hot with steamed rice.

VARIATIONS Try tofu in place of the chicken. Use firm tofu cut into 1-inch cubes. Chunks of halibut or another firm white-fleshed fish would work well, too.

HEADS UP

The dish calls for Fresh Green Curry Paste (page 33). You can prepare it up to 3 days ahead.

Khao Man Gai

 SERVES 4

If you've ever tasted this Thai specialty, you understand the simple, yet utterly addictive nature of the dish. Poached chicken (bone-in to keep it moist) rests quietly on a mound of garlicky jasmine rice— a bit boring on its own—until a blast of punchy ginger sauce brings it to life. Traditionally, the sauce includes a thick yellow Thai soybean sauce, but I couldn't find any gluten-free brands. I substitute miso paste for the bean sauce and while not authentic, it's still delicious. The ginger sauce, cucumber, and cilantro are essential to the outcome of the dish. Please don't leave them out. I like to poach the chicken and then use the flavorful cooking liquid to make the rice in the same pan. To save about 15 minutes, though, you can cook the chicken and rice simultaneously, but you will need an extra 2 cups of chicken broth to cook the rice.

2 cups store-bought **GF** or home-made chicken broth (page 37)

3 (¼-inch-thick) slices unpeeled fresh ginger

2 pounds bone-in chicken breasts

1 teaspoon vegetable oil

3 cloves garlic, minced

1½ cups jasmine rice

½ teaspoon salt

1 English cucumber, thinly sliced, for serving

1 cup loosely packed cilantro leaves, for serving

Fiery Ginger Sauce (page 30), for serving

HEADS UP

The dish calls for Fiery Ginger Sauce (page 30). You can prepare it up to 3 days ahead.

In a medium saucepan, bring the chicken broth and ginger to a boil. Add the chicken and simmer gently (do not boil), turning the chicken once, for 15 minutes. (The chicken may not be submerged. That is not a problem as long as you turn it.) Turn the chicken once more, bring the liquid just back to a simmer, and then cover the pan. Turn off the heat and steam the chicken until just cooked through, about 15 minutes longer, depending on the thickness of the chicken. Transfer the chicken to a cutting board, remove and discard the ginger, and set aside the broth. Let the chicken cool for a few minutes before slicing. You want the chicken to be moist and just cooked; do not cover the chicken or it will continue cooking. The chicken will keep, covered, in the refrigerator for up to 2 days. Bring it to room temperature before serving.

Pour the cooking liquid into a large measuring cup and wipe out the pan. If needed, add enough water to equal 2 cups of liquid. Heat the oil in the pan over medium heat. Add the garlic and cook until sizzling, about 1 minute. Add the rice and stir to coat with the oil. Stir in the chicken broth and salt and bring to a boil. Lower the heat and simmer, covered, for

(continued)

(continued from page 155)

12 minutes. Remove the pan from the heat and steam the rice, covered, for 5 minutes.

For serving, pull the skin off the chicken, remove the chicken from the bone with your fingers, and cut it into approximately $^1/_3$-inch-thick slices. Spoon a mound of rice onto the center of each plate; top the rice with some of the chicken (or present the dish on a platter, family style) and the cucumber and cilantro. Serve the chicken and rice warm or at room temperature with the ginger sauce spooned over the top.

Japanese-Style Chicken Curry *with Potatoes and Carrots*

 SERVES 4

Japanese chicken curries often contain "curry roux," a mixture of wheat flour, oil, and curry powder used to thicken the stew. As a gluten-free option, I thicken my sauce by simmering it uncovered for the final minutes to concentrate the flavors, and then whisk in a cornstarch slurry to finish the job. Unlike Thai curries, which are based on fresh curry pastes, this one uses a curry powder. S&B Oriental curry powder contains an intriguing combination of spices (fenugreek, star anise, nutmeg), or you can try another brand you feel comfortable using, even an Indian garam masala. The flavor and heat level will change depending on the spice blend you use; you may need to add more honey or salt to taste.

2 tablespoons vegetable oil

8 chicken drumsticks (about 3 pounds)

3 carrots, peeled and cut into 1-inch pieces

1 pound potatoes, peeled and cut into 1$^1/_2$-inch chunks (2 medium potatoes)

1 onion, thinly sliced

3 cloves garlic, minced

In a large frying pan, heat the oil over medium-high heat. Sprinkle the chicken with a large pinch of salt. Cook the chicken, in batches if necessary, turning occasionally, until browned, about 5 minutes. As the chicken browns, transfer it to a Dutch oven or a large, heavy pot. Add the carrots and potatoes to the Dutch oven.

When all the chicken is browned, add the onion to the frying pan and cook until starting to soften, about 5 minutes. Stir in the garlic, ginger, and curry powder and cook 1 minute

2 tablespoons minced fresh ginger

1½ tablespoons curry powder

3 cups store-bought GF or homemade chicken broth (page 37)

1¼ teaspoons salt

2 teaspoons soy sauce or tamari GF

1 teaspoon honey

1 teaspoon cornstarch

1 tablespoon cold water

Steamed rice, for serving

longer. Add the chicken broth and bring to a simmer, scraping up any browned bits from the bottom of the pan. Pour the onion mixture over the chicken legs. Add the salt and bring to a simmer. Simmer, partially covered, for 30 minutes, turning the chicken pieces occasionally. Remove the lid and simmer until the chicken, carrots, and potatoes are tender and the sauce starts to thicken, about 10 minutes longer. Stir in the soy sauce and honey.

Mix together the cornstarch and cold water in a small bowl and then stir it into the simmering sauce. Simmer until the sauce thickens, about 2 minutes. Serve the curry hot with steamed rice. You can make the curry ahead; cool to room temperature and then refrigerate it, covered, for up to 2 days. Reheat it in a pan on top of the stove.

VARIATIONS You can use bone-in chicken breasts and cut back the cooking time by about 10 minutes. But be sure to use bone-in chicken; it adds both flavor and a home-style feeling to the dish.

A cup or so of drained canned chickpeas would be a great addition as well.

Soy Sauce Chicken

 SERVES 4

When it comes to easy family-friendly recipes, this dish tops the list. You basically toss the ingredients in a pot, forming a super flavorful poaching liquid. Simmer the chicken for a bit and then set the whole thing aside to finish cooking and infuse with flavor for an hour or two while you grab the kids from school. You can even reuse the poaching liquid to cook more chicken for another meal. Just strain the cooking liquid and refrigerate it for up to 1 week or freeze it for up to 1 month. Serve the chicken with rice or shredded and wrapped in warm Mandarin pancakes (page 68).

---

2 cups soy sauce or tamari **GF**

2 cups store-bought **GF** or homemade chicken broth (page 37)

1/2 cup dry sherry or Chinese Shaoxing rice wine **GF**

2/3 cup packed brown sugar

3 (1/4-inch-thick) slices unpeeled fresh ginger

4 teaspoons Chinese five-spice powder

3 cloves garlic, smashed

1 teaspoon black peppercorns

31/2 pounds bone-in chicken thighs

Steamed rice, for serving

....

HEADS UP
You'll need to cool the chicken for at least 1 hour and up to 3 hours.

In a pot large enough to hold the chicken, combine the soy sauce, chicken broth, sherry, brown sugar, ginger, five-spice powder, garlic, and peppercorns. Bring to a boil. Lower the heat and simmer to combine the flavors, about 15 minutes.

Add the chicken to the broth and simmer for 10 minutes. Turn the chicken pieces over with tongs and simmer 10 minutes longer. Remove the pot from the heat and let the chicken stand, covered, for at least 1 hour, and up to 3 hours, to gently finish the cooking. (For food safety reasons, do not leave it at room temperature for longer than 3 hours.)

Serve the chicken at room temperature with a small bowl of the poaching liquid for drizzling over the chicken and rice. Or refrigerate the chicken in its poaching liquid for up to 1 day and serve it cold or reheat it. If you want to save the poaching liquid for cooking more chicken, strain it into a container and refrigerate it, covered, for up to 1 week or freeze it for about 1 month. Bring the liquid to a boil for several minutes before using it again.

VARIATIONS You can use boneless chicken thighs instead of bone-in. Simmer them for 6 to 8 minutes per side.

Instead of the chicken, cut a 3- to 4-pound piece of boneless pork shoulder into 11/2-inch chunks. Add the meat to the broth and simmer gently, partially covered, until tender, about 11/2 hours, then follow the recipe, adding a bit of salt (to the meat, not the broth) if needed.

Japanese Pub Fried Chicken

 SERVES 4 AS A MAIN DISH, 6 AS AN APPETIZER

I rarely deep-fry, but when the urge strikes, my kids go absolutely nuts over this chicken. A thin coating of cornstarch replaces any heavy batter, keeping things light. Traditionally, a squeeze of lemon over the top is all you need, but my son loves to sprinkle shichimi togarashi *over anything vaguely Japanese—I have to hand it to him, the combination of chile pepper, dried tangerine peel, nori, and sesame seeds (among others) tastes great on the chicken. You can find it in the spice section of Asian markets or the Asian section of upscale grocery stores. Serve the chicken with steamed edamame.*

1¹/₂ pounds boneless, skinless chicken thighs, cut into 1¹/₂-inch chunks

3 tablespoons mirin

3 tablespoons soy sauce or tamari **GF**

3 cloves garlic, minced

Vegetable oil, for frying

¹/₃ cup cornstarch

Salt

Lemon wedges, for serving

Shichimi togarashi (see page 17), for serving (optional)

HEADS UP
You'll need to marinate the chicken for at least 30 minutes and up to 4 hours.

Put the chicken in a bowl and toss with the mirin, soy sauce, and garlic. Let the chicken marinate for at least 30 minutes or up to 4 hours in the refrigerator. Drain the chicken in a colander over the sink and then return it to the bowl.

In a wok or a medium saucepan, heat about 3 inches of oil to 350°F over medium heat. This may take about 15 minutes. (If you don't have a deep-fry thermometer, sprinkle a bit of cornstarch in the oil. When it sizzles vigorously, it's ready. The oil should not get hot enough to smoke.) Add the cornstarch to the chicken and toss with a fork to coat. Line a plate with paper towels. Carefully add about one-quarter of the chicken to the oil, a few pieces at a time to avoid splattering. Cook the chicken, stirring occasionally to keep the pieces from sticking together, until brown and cooked through, about 6 minutes per batch. Remove the chicken from the oil with a slotted spoon and transfer it to the prepared plate. Sprinkle the chicken with a pinch of salt while it is hot. Cook the remaining chicken in two or three more batches, returning the oil to 350°F before cooking each batch. Serve the chicken immediately, or keep it warm in a low oven. For serving, squeeze a bit of lemon and some *shichimi togarishi* over the chicken.

VARIATION You can use boneless, skinless chicken breasts instead of the thighs. The white meat will cook faster, about 4 to 5 minutes per batch.

While exploring the different options for preparing meat, I found myself almost exclusively focusing on beef and pork. Many Asian cooks include small bits of pork in a vast array of dishes, and personally I can't think of a better condiment. The meat recipes in this chapter are sized as main dishes, but there are recipes throughout the book that follow this idea of using a small quantity of meat for a burst of flavor. Even though I enjoy eating meat, sometimes a little taste is enough to satisfy.

If you haven't shopped in the meat department of an Asian grocery before, put it on your to-do list. They offer specialty cuts of meat that regular groceries don't carry: thinly sliced rib-eye steak for *bulgogi*, bacon-thin slices of pork belly or side pork for Spicy Pork with Kimchi and Tofu, and stubby little lengths of short ribs for Asian Braised Short Ribs are among my favorite finds. Using these cuts is certainly not essential for a successful dish, but I find them to be time-savers (less cutting) that make the meal seem a bit more authentic.

Many meat dishes convert to gluten free with a simple substitution of gluten-free soy sauce or hoisin sauce; others take a bit more maneuvering. Pork Tonkatsu, normally covered in a panko-breadcrumb crust, stays true to its nature in a new cornflake coating. I skip the flour-dusting of my short ribs, thickening the sauce instead with a bit of cornstarch. And as for the Mu Shu Pork, I knew that just wouldn't be the same without the Mandarin pancakes (page 68).

Shaking Beef

 SERVES 4

Some upscale Vietnamese restaurants serve shaking beef, a special (read: expensive) dish combining seared steak with a peppery watercress salad. Filet mignon is often the meat of choice, though I like strip steak for its beefy flavor and (slightly) lower price tag. Leave the meat alone in the pan for a full 2 minutes—no poking or prodding—and then shake the pan back and forth to flip the meat. You want the steak medium-rare; it should be in and out of the pan pretty quickly. Please note that several of the ingredients are used in both the marinade and the dressing; keep an eye on the correct quantities.

---

2 pounds boneless New York strip steak or other steak, cut into approximately 1¹/₂-inch cubes

4 cloves garlic, minced

1¹/₂ tablespoons plus 4 teaspoons soy sauce or tamari GF, divided

1¹/₂ teaspoons plus 1 tablespoon sugar, divided

1¹/₂ teaspoons salt, divided

1 teaspoon freshly ground black pepper, divided

¹/₄ cup freshly squeezed lime juice

4 tablespoons vegetable oil, divided

Half a small red onion, thinly sliced

1 tablespoon unseasoned rice vinegar

2 bunches watercress (6 to 8 ounces total), large stems removed

1 cup halved cherry tomatoes

To marinate the beef, put the beef in a bowl and toss it with the garlic, 1¹/₂ tablespoons of the soy sauce, 1¹/₂ teaspoons of the sugar, 1 teaspoon of the salt, and ¹/₂ teaspoon of the black pepper. Let the meat marinate at room temperature while preparing the remaining ingredients.

In a small bowl, whisk together the lime juice, 2 tablespoons of the vegetable oil, and the remaining 4 teaspoons of soy sauce, 1 tablespoon sugar, ¹/₂ teaspoon salt, and ¹/₂ teaspoon black pepper. Set aside.

In a small bowl, toss the onion with the rice vinegar. Transfer the watercress to a serving platter and top with the tomatoes and the onion mixture.

In a large frying pan, heat 1 tablespoon of the oil over medium-high heat. Add half the beef to the pan and cook for 2 minutes without touching it. Shake the pan vigorously to turn the beef (thus "shaking beef"), or if you want, just use tongs to turn the meat. Continue cooking until the meat is medium-rare, 1 to 2 minutes longer. Put the cooked beef on top of the bed of watercress. Repeat with the remaining beef and 1 tablespoon oil. Stir the dressing and drizzle about half of it over the meat and salad. Pass the remaining dressing at the table. Serve hot or at room temperature.

VARIATION You can substitute baby spinach or a mesclun mix for the watercress, though this will significantly change the character of the dish, losing the peppery bite of the watercress.

Stir-Fried Beef with Basil

 SERVES 2 TO 4

If you come across Thai basil or holy basil at an Asian market, try it in this stir-fry for an authentic and interesting flavor. Otherwise, regular basil or cilantro will do just fine. Try not to overload the pan or the meat will steam; I purposely kept the quantities small to prevent pan overload. You'll need a few side dishes if you want to serve four, or double the quantities, but be sure to cook the stir-fry in two separate batches.

1 tablespoon vegetable oil

1/2 onion, thinly sliced (about 1 cup)

1 red jalapeño chile, thinly sliced

1/2 green bell pepper, thinly sliced (about 1/2 cup)

1/4 pound green beans, cut into 3/4-inch lengths (about 1 cup)

3/4 pound ground beef

1 1/2 teaspoons sugar

1 tablespoon Asian fish sauce

1 tablespoon soy sauce or tamari GF

1/2 cup Thai basil, cilantro, or regular basil

Steamed rice, for serving (optional)

In a large frying pan or a wok, heat the oil over medium-high heat. Add the onion, jalapeño, green bell pepper, and green beans and cook, stirring frequently, until the vegetables start to soften, about 4 minutes. Raise the heat to high. Add the ground beef and cook, breaking the meat up with a spoon, until it is no longer pink, about 3 minutes. Stir in the sugar and cook 1 minute longer. Add the fish sauce, soy sauce, and basil. Remove the pan from the heat and toss to combine. Serve over steamed rice.

VARIATIONS You can use ground pork, chicken, or even lamb instead of the beef.

Bulgogi

 SERVES 4

Bulgogi is often the "gateway dish" introducing many Americans to the pleasures of Korean cooking. These thin slices of marinated beef, also known as Korean barbecue, are often grilled tabletop at Korean restaurants, but I find this dish just as delicious hot out of a skillet. The meat develops a nicer crust in a regular pan, but you can also use nonstick for easier cleanup. Asian markets (specifically Korean or Japanese) cut the meat in very thin slices specifically for this dish. If it's hard to find this cut, freeze whole boneless rib-eye steaks just until they start to firm up, about 20 minutes, for easier slicing. Serve bulgogi with steamed rice, wrapped in lettuce with a dollop of hot sauce, or even rolled in rice paper wrappers. Bulgogi is an ingredient or a variation in several other recipes in this book, so it's a good idea to make extra for multiple meals (see below).

1/3 cup soy sauce **or** tamari **GF**

3 cloves garlic, minced

2 tablespoons sugar

1 1/2 tablespoons toasted sesame oil

1 tablespoon sake

1/2 teaspoon freshly ground black pepper

1 1/2 pounds boneless rib-eye steak, very thinly sliced for bulgogi

HEADS UP
You'll need to marinate the meat for at least 1 hour and up to 24 hours.
You can freeze the marinated meat in 1/2 pound batches for up to a month. Defrost in the fridge before using

In a small bowl, combine the soy sauce, garlic, sugar, sesame oil, sake, and pepper. Mix well to combine. Put the meat in a glass baking dish or a gallon-size resealable bag. Add the marinade and toss to coat. Refrigerate, covered, for at least 1 hour or up to 24 hours. More time equals more flavor.

Heat a large frying pan over medium-high heat. Add as much meat to the pan as will fit without overcrowding (you want the meat to brown, not steam) and cook, stirring occasionally, until browned and cooked through, 3 to 5 minutes. Remove the meat from the pan and transfer it to a plate. Repeat with the remaining meat.

VARIATIONS Instead of thinly sliced rib-eye, Asian markets also sell thin beef short ribs known as *kalbi*. Follow the marinating directions above and grill the ribs until brown and cooked through, about 4 minutes per side. Keep the heat moderate or the sugar in the marinade will burn. You can also marinate whole rib-eye steaks and grill them. Again, just watch the heat.

Bulgogi is also an ingredient or a variation in Salad Rolls with Crab and Spicy Mango Sauce (page 51), Korean-Style Chicken Tacos (page 49), Vietnamese Rice Noodle Salad (page 84), Sweet Potato Noodles with Beef and Vegetables (page 91), Spring Vegetable Fried Rice (page 104), Bibimbap (page 108), and Stir-Fried Rice Cakes with Shrimp and Vegetables (page 110).

Asian Braised Short Ribs

 SERVES 4

Whenever the weather even hints at chilly, my husband requests "something braised." If you've braised short ribs before, the technique here is the same, but the flavors change to add a distinctive Asian flair. The star anise contributes a warm licorice note to the ribs. Find it at upscale markets or Asian groceries. Butchers in Asian markets sell short ribs in 3-inch segments. If your market doesn't offer this option, go ahead and cook the full-size version. Serve the ribs with steamed rice, or simmer soaked cellophane noodles directly in the sauce to soak up the flavor.

---

1 tablespoon vegetable oil

4 pounds beef short ribs

2 teaspoons salt

8 cloves garlic, smashed

4 quarter-size slices unpeeled fresh ginger

2 cups water

1/2 cup soy sauce or tamari **GF**

1/2 cup dry sherry or Shaoxing rice wine **GF**

2 tablespoons brown sugar

1 tablespoon unseasoned rice vinegar

2 whole star anise

1/2 ounce dried shiitake mushrooms, soaked in warm water for 15 minutes

1 pound turnips, peeled and cut into 1-inch wedges (about 2 cups)

2 teaspoons cornstarch mixed with 1 tablespoon cold water (optional)

Heat the oil in a large frying pan over medium-high heat. Pat the ribs dry with a paper towel and then sprinkle them with the salt. Brown the ribs well on all sides, 6 to 8 minutes per batch. Transfer the ribs to a plate.

While the ribs are browning, combine the garlic, ginger, water, soy sauce, sherry, brown sugar, rice vinegar, and star anise in a Dutch oven or a pot large enough to hold the ribs. Remove the mushrooms from the soaking liquid and, if they are whole, cut them into thin slices. Add them to the Dutch oven and bring the liquid to a simmer. Add the ribs to the pot. Return the liquid to a simmer. Simmer the ribs gently, partially covered, until almost tender, about 1 hour. Turn the ribs occasionally with tongs during cooking.

Add the turnip cubes to the pot; make sure they are covered in the liquid. Bring the liquid back to a simmer. Cook, partially covered, until the turnips and meat are tender, 15 to 20 minutes longer.

With a slotted spoon, transfer the meat and vegetables to a deep serving casserole. Degrease the sauce by pouring it through a fat separator or by tilting the pot and spooning off the oil that accumulates on the surface. Bring the sauce to a low boil and cook until it reduces slightly, about 10 minutes. At this point you can pour the sauce over the meat or thicken it with the cornstarch mixture. Stir the cornstarch into the simmering

(continued)

(continued from page 167)

sauce and cook until thickened, 1 to 2 minutes. Serve hot or cool and refrigerate, covered, for up to 2 days.

VARIATIONS You can make this recipe into more of a stew by using 3 pounds of boneless beef chuck cut into 1¹/₂-inch cubes, or 3- to 4-pound brisket. The whole cut will take longer to cook, possibly a few hours depending on the size. Check for doneness by inserting the tip of a paring knife into the meat, it should slide in and out easily.

Spicy Pork *with Kimchi and Tofu*

 SERVES 4

If couples are allowed a signature dish, this one belongs to my husband and me. Something about the combination of sweet, tart, and spicy makes it so crave-worthy; we even like reheating leftovers for breakfast. Meat departments in Asian markets generally carry fresh pork belly or side pork, sliced "bacon thin" for this dish. If you can't find either of these cuts, use uncured sliced bacon. The dish is a light main dish for 4; serve it with rice and a vegetable or two.

1 pound firm tofu

1 tablespoon vegetable oil

6 green onions, white and green parts, thinly sliced, divided

¹/₂ pound thinly sliced pork belly or side pork, cut crosswise into ¹/₂-inch strips

2 cups coarsely chopped kimchi **GF**, plus 1 to 2 tablespoons of liquid

1 tablespoon soy sauce or tamari **GF**

2 teaspoons Korean chili powder, or substitute 2 teaspoons paprika with a pinch of cayenne pepper

2 teaspoons sugar

1¹/₂ teaspoons toasted sesame oil

1 tablespoon toasted sesame seeds

Steamed rice, for serving (optional)

Put the tofu in a small saucepan with cold water to cover. Bring the water just to a boil. Lower the heat and simmer until the tofu is heated through, about 5 minutes. Remove the pan from the heat.

Meanwhile, in a large frying pan or a wok, heat the oil over medium-high heat. Add the green onion whites and cook, stirring, for 1 minute. Add the pork and cook, stirring occasionally, until starting to brown (but not crisp), about 5 minutes. Stir in the kimchi and its liquid, the soy sauce, chili powder, and sugar and cook until heated through, about 5 minutes. Transfer the pork and kimchi to a platter. Top with the green-onion greens, sesame oil, and sesame seeds.

Remove the tofu from the water and drain on paper towels or a clean kitchen towel. Cut the tofu in half lengthwise and then cut crosswise into ¹/₂-inch slices. Put the tofu slices on the platter surrounding the pork and kimchi. Serve hot with steamed rice.

Chinese Barbecued Pork

 SERVES 4 TO 6

The neon-red barbecued pork you see in Chinese restaurants generally gets its color from red food coloring. I like to keep things a bit more natural, so I removed the artificial coloring along with the gluten. The pork should be in narrow strips to ensure the marinade penetrates every bite. The strips roast quickly in the oven, but you could also cook them on the grill. Use leftovers as a fantastic addition to Spring Vegetable Fried Rice (page 104).

1/4 cup hoisin sauce GF

3 tablespoons soy sauce or tamari GF

3 tablespoons sake

2 tablespoons sugar

2 cloves garlic, minced

1/2 teaspoon Chinese five-spice powder

2 pounds pork tenderloin

1/2 teaspoon salt

2 tablespoons honey

HEADS UP
You'll need to marinate the pork for at least 4 hours and up to 36 hours.

In a small bowl, stir together the hoisin sauce, soy sauce, sake, sugar, garlic, and five-spice powder. If the pork is thicker than 2 inches, cut it in half lengthwise. Poke the pork in several places with a fork so the marinade will penetrate. Transfer the pork strips to a glass baking dish or a gallon-size resealable bag and pour the marinade over the pork. Turn to coat the pieces evenly. Refrigerate the pork, covered, for at least 4 hours and up to 36 hours. More time equals more flavor.

Heat the oven to 425°F. Line a baking sheet with foil to keep the honey from burning on the pan. Transfer the pork to the baking sheet; discard the extra marinade. Sprinkle the pork with the salt. Cook for 15 minutes. Brush the pork with the honey and then continue cooking until the pork is cooked through (138°F to 140°F on a meat thermometer), 15 to 20 minutes longer depending on the thickness of the pork. Let the pork stand for about 15 minutes before cutting into approximately 1/4 inch slices. Serve warm or at room temperature.

Mu Shu Pork

 SERVES 4

If you want to hone your knife skills, preparing the vegetables for this stir-fry will give you tons of practice. The idea is to cut everything in a similar shape, in this case long and thin, not only to promote even cooking but also for looks. Have everything prepared and ready to go before you start cooking: once the first piece of food hits the pan, things move fast. The mu shu tastes great wrapped in Mandarin pancakes with a dab of hoisin sauce or in steamed corn tortillas for an easy alternative. Although I do not purport tortillas to be a remotely authentic substitute, they still taste good. The wood ear provides a chewy, almost gelatinous texture to the dish. Although very different, you could soak 1/3 cup dried shiitake mushrooms and use them.

1 pound boneless pork loin or boneless center-cut pork chops

3 tablespoons soy sauce or tamari **GF**, divided

2 tablespoons sake, dry sherry, or Shaoxing rice wine **GF**

1¹/₂ teaspoons cornstarch

4 tablespoons vegetable oil, divided

2 eggs, beaten with a pinch of salt

4 cloves garlic, minced

6 green onions, white parts only, thinly sliced

¹/₃ cup wood ear (also called dried black fungus), soaked in warm water for 15 minutes, squeezed dry, and shredded

2 cups shredded cabbage

¹/₂ cup drained and rinsed canned bamboo shoots, shredded lengthwise

¹/₄ teaspoon salt

Hoisin sauce **GF**, for serving

Mandarin pancakes (page 68) or small corn tortillas, for serving

Cut the pork loin into 4 chunks and put it in the freezer for 20 to 30 minutes. (You want to slice the pork really thin and regardless of your knife skills, this will make it easier.) Cut the pork into ¹/₄-inch-thick slices. Stack the slices and cut the meat into thin strips. Toss the pork with 2 tablespoons of the soy sauce, the sake, and the cornstarch. Set aside to marinate while you prepare the remaining ingredients.

In a large frying pan or a wok, heat 1 tablespoon of the oil over medium-high heat. Add the eggs and let them set until puffy, about 30 seconds. Scramble the eggs just until cooked through and transfer them to a large bowl. Return the pan to high heat and add 1 tablespoon of the oil. Add half the pork and cook, without stirring, for 30 seconds. Stir the pork and then continue cooking, stirring occasionally, until cooked through, about 3 minutes. Transfer the pork to the bowl with the eggs. Repeat with the remaining pork and 1 tablespoon oil.

Heat the remaining 1 tablespoon oil in the pan over medium-high heat. Add the garlic and green onions and cook, stirring, for 30 seconds. Add the wood ear, cabbage, and bamboo shoots and cook, stirring occasionally, until the cabbage starts to wilt, about 3 minutes. Add the pork and eggs back to the pan and toss to combine. Stir in the remaining 1 tablespoon

(continued)

(continued from page 170)

HEADS UP

You'll need to freeze the pork for 20 to 30 minutes for slicing. This dish calls for Mandarin pancakes (page 68). You can make them up to 2 days ahead, stored in the refrigerator, or freeze them for up to 1 month.

soy sauce and the salt; cook until heated through, 1 to 2 minutes longer. For serving, spread a spoonful of hoisin sauce on a warm Mandarin pancake or a corn tortilla. (Just before serving, steam them for 10 minutes over simmering water or wrap the stack of pancakes or tortillas in a barely damp paper towel and then plastic wrap and microwave them until hot.) Top with the mu shu pork and roll it up.

VARIATION You can substitute boneless chicken thighs or breast for the pork.

Pork Tonkatsu

 SERVES 4

When I stopped eating gluten, I also temporarily stopped serving my kids one of their favorite Japanese meals, tonkatsu. Luckily, I found a way to reintroduce the breaded pork (or chicken) cutlets by coating them with cornflake crumbs instead of the usual panko breadcrumbs. Just be sure to use gluten-free cornflakes; those containing barley malt as a sweetener are not gluten free. You can crush the cornflakes into crumbs in a resealable bag. I include two very different ways to serve the pork, one with a simple dipping sauce and another (listed as a variation) with a quick sauce of soy-simmered onions and egg. Both versions work well with steamed rice.

1/3 cup ketchup

4 teaspoons soy sauce or tamari **GF**

1 tablespoon sugar

1 tablespoon Worcestershire sauce **GF**

1 1/2 teaspoons grated fresh ginger

Pinch of ground allspice

To make the dipping sauce, combine the ketchup, soy sauce, sugar, Worcestershire sauce, ginger, and allspice in a small bowl. Stir to combine. The sauce can be made up to 1 week ahead and stored, covered, in the refrigerator.

1/2 cup cornstarch

2 eggs

1 1/2 cups cornflakes **GF**, crushed into crumbs

4 boneless pork chops (about 6 ounces each), pounded to a 1/2-inch thickness

3/4 teaspoon salt

1/4 teaspoon freshly ground black pepper

3 tablespoons vegetable oil, plus more if needed

Shredded cabbage, for serving

Lemon wedges, for serving

Set three wide bowls or rimmed plates on the counter. (They should be wide enough to hold a pork chop.) Pour the cornstarch into one bowl. Beat the eggs in another, and pour the cornflake crumbs into the last bowl. Sprinkle the pork with the salt and pepper. One at a time, coat a pork chop with the cornstarch, shaking any excess back into the bowl. Dip the pork chop into the egg and then coat it with cornflake crumbs. As you finish, transfer the pork chop to a wire rack. Repeat with the remaining pork chops. The pork chops can be coated a few hours ahead of time. Keep them on the wire rack set over a baking sheet or a plate, refrigerated, until ready to cook.

In a large nonstick frying pan, heat 1 1/2 tablespoons of the oil over medium heat. Add as many pork chops as will fit in the pan and cook, turning once, until the pork chops are cooked through, 3 to 4 minutes per side for 1/2-inch-thick chops. Repeat with the remaining pork chops and oil. Serve the pork chops with the dipping sauce, cabbage, and a squeeze of lemon juice.

VARIATIONS To make a dish called *katsudon*: Replace the dipping sauce in this recipe with 1 cup chicken broth **GF**, 1/4 cup soy sauce **GF**, 5 tablespoons mirin, and 1 small thinly sliced onion in a small saucepan. Simmer for 10 minutes. Stir in 2 beaten eggs and simmer until the eggs are cooked, about 2 minutes. Serve the pork sliced over steamed rice and top with the sauce.

Substitute boneless, skinless chicken breasts for the pork chops. Pound them to a 1/2-inch thickness.

ELEVEN Sips and Sweets

You may find the final chapter of the book to be a bit, *ahem*, nontraditional. Although I am generally a very ambitious eater, my taste buds just haven't adapted to many of the classic Asian desserts, often containing things like beans and corn. In the meantime, I decided to construct an Asian-inspired list that plays well to my tastes. What I do love are fruit-based desserts, presented here as a simple Lychee Sorbet, Mango with Sweet Rice and Coconut Sauce, and a drop-dead delicious dairy-free Coconut Ice Cream. Pushing the envelope a bit more, I developed a tasty berry crisp, completely American in nature if not for an exotic note of Chinese five-spice powder in the topping. And for a real crowd-pleaser, try the Thai Coffee Macarons—light-as-air cocoa and almond-flour cookies sandwiched around a chocolate-and-coffee ganache. They are deliciously reminiscent of, well, Thai coffee.

On the beverage front, I've included a unique lineup of both cocktails and refreshing nonalcoholic drinks. Once you make the spicy ginger syrup for Sparkling Ginger Limeade, you will always want to have some around. Blueberry Drinking Vinegar, a concoction I first tasted in Tokyo, causes instant addiction and possibly even a new hobby. And if you spy a bottle of Japanese plum wine in the grocery store, turn it into a crisp, fruity Plum Wine Sangria, perfect for a warm summer day.

Generally, if I imbibe while enjoying an Asian meal, I turn to sake (see Exploring Sake: A Primer, page 176). The quality and availability of fine sake is increasing at lightning speed. Asian markets generally carry a wide assortment of sakes, and although the supply is more limited at grocery and wine stores—usually only a few choices—the overall market is growing. (By the way, you should look for sake in the wine section, not in a condiment aisle.) If you haven't come to appreciate the joys of sake, I highly recommend a little exploration, especially considering its naturally gluten-free status. Like anything that tastes delicious in its pure state, I hesitate to add flavors to sake, but having said that, it does make an awfully tasty Blackberry Sake Mojito or Cucumber Saketini.

Exploring Sake: A Primer

By Marcus Pakiser

Have you ever tasted a wine you didn't like? Did that isolated sip make you give up on wine forever? If a single "jet fuel" experience with sake tainted your impression, hold the final judgment until you sample some more of this alluring brew.

Sake (pronounced sah-KAY) is an alcoholic beverage brewed from polished rice; it is not distilled. The term "brewing" may lead you to think of rice beer, but sake is neither wine nor beer, but in a category of its own. Sake ferments to about 20 percent alcohol, and is subsequently diluted to a final concentration of about 15 to 16 percent alcohol. Sake is 100 percent gluten free and sulfite free.

Categories of Sake

Fats and proteins comprise the outer layers of a grain of rice. These layers can adversely affect fermentation, causing off flavors in the final brew. To combat this problem, the rice is "polished" prior to brewing, removing these outer layers to varying degrees. The level of polishing determines the quality level of the sake. The more the rice is polished, the smaller the grain becomes. Removing the fats and proteins and leaving only the starch center paves the way for crafting a higher quality sake. A sake with 55 percent polish means that 45 percent of the grain has been removed. A 35 percent polish means 65 percent of the grain has been removed. Levels of sake are based on this polish ratio.

Daiginjo: Sake with at least 50 percent or more of the rice grain polished away prior to brewing. This represents the highest level of sake and offers an extremely delicate, fruity, and silky smooth flavor. *Daiginjo* sake should only be served chilled.

Ginjo: Sake with a polish ratio of 50 to 60 percent (50 to 40 percent of the grain removed). *Ginjo*-level sake offers a wide variety of flavors that can be expressive, fruity, and rich; it should be served chilled.

Junmai: Sake that is brewed with rice, water, yeast, and *koji*—an enzyme. *Junmai* sake can be any polish ratio, but that ratio must appear on the bottle. *Junmai* sake can be served chilled or many can be gently heated to body temperature. It should not be hot. Most *junmai* sake in the United States is 60 to 70 percent polished. Once it reaches a *ginjo* or *daiginjo* level, the sake is referred to as *junmai ginjo* or *junmai daiginjo*.

Honjozo: Any sake with a bit of brewers' alcohol added to the mash at the end of fermentation. This process adds flavor and aroma to the sake. *Honjozo* styles result in a light-bodied sake. Some *honjozo* can be heated to body temperature.

Nigori: A "cloudy" sake, due to some of the rice sediment from the fermentation being allowed to remain in the brew. *Nigori* sake must be shaken before serving it chilled. Though there are a few drier versions on the market, most *nigori* sake is sweeter than other types of sake.

Pairing with Food

The Japanese saying "*Nihonshu wa tabemono to erabanai*" means "Sake doesn't get into a fight with the food." Pairing sake only with sushi or sashimi is like limiting Italian wine to a spaghetti dinner. Sake pairs well with seafood; the right amount of acidity enhances the richness and flavor of the fish without overwhelming it like a great big wine could do. Earthy sake works well with meats, mushrooms, and richer dishes. The earthy sakes, which tend to be on the dry side, support the flavor of these dishes without getting lost. A surprising pairing matches sake with cheese. Sake adds a background to the cheese, subtly enhancing its richness without a fight like some wines can put up. Getting past preconceived notions of serving sake only with Japanese food will open up a world of possibilities.

Some Misconceptions about Sake

"Sake should be served hot." Not true; in fact, almost never. The hot sake found in some restaurants is low-end sake. Once upon a time, Japanese companies would only export their lowest quality sake, keeping the best for themselves. Not anymore. Today, many restaurants carry twenty to fifty sakes on their list, one to serve warm and the rest premium sakes to be served chilled. Heating premium sake makes as much sense as serving a hot chardonnay. As previously mentioned, there are a few sakes that can be served warm, but to body temperature, not coffee-hot.

"All sake is the same." Not true. As you taste, look for different qualities such as dry, earthy, rich and penetrating, light and fruity. Sake is as diverse as wine; some is crafted with strong sake yeast, creating bold, robust flavor. Other sake uses flower yeast (*hana kobo*), yielding an elegant, floral aroma and delicate flavor.

"Sake gives you a terrible hangover." Not true. Of course, the low-grade, hot box sake or excessive consumption of any alcohol can cause a headache or dehydration. Premium sake is kind on the system because many of the proteins have been removed and it contains no sulfites. Because sake is usually enjoyed unadorned, the problems caused by mixing different types of alcohol or using sugary mixers are eliminated as well. Always drink plenty of water when you consume any alcohol.

When you venture out to buy sake, be aware that it does have a shelf life. If you see a date on the bottle, it's best to purchase one less than eighteen months old. Unlike wine, sake is not meant to withstand long aging. Think of it more like beer—the fresher the better. Purchase sake from a store with a large selection that rotates its stock frequently.

Once you open a bottle of sake it will stay fresh for at least a month or two; premium sake may last up to four months. Although it is best to keep opened bottles well capped in the refrigerator, this is only mandatory for unpasteurized (*nama*) sake. Try this amazing, gluten-free beverage with your next meal.

Marcus's Picks

Most of the following are available nationwide and will make great starting points for your new investigation of sake.

Momokawa Organic Junmai Ginjo
Fukucho "Moon on the Water" Junmai Ginjo
Watari Bune Junmai Ginjo 55
G Joy
Eiko Fuji Ban Ryu

—*Marcus Pakiser has eighteen years in the sake business, both as a sake brewer and as a national sales manager and distributor of sake. He has led hundreds of sake seminars and training sessions as well as penned the sake menus for hundreds of restaurants nationwide. He currently manages the Sake category for P&S Wine Company, a division of Young's Columbia Oregon.*

Sparkling Ginger Limeade

 SERVES 6 TO 8

For this ultra-refreshing summer cooler, a ginger simple syrup is mixed with fresh lime juice and a splash of sparkling water. With a batch of ginger syrup in the refrigerator, you have a stealth secret weapon at your disposal. It makes a stellar addition to cocktails, from gin and tonics to whiskey sours. Toss it with sliced strawberries or peaches as a topping for waffles or ice cream, or use it to enhance iced tea.

6 ounces unpeeled fresh ginger, rinsed and cut into 1/4-inch-thick slices

3/4 cup light agave nectar

1 1/2 cups water

3/4 cup freshly squeezed lime juice

3 cups sparkling water or club soda

HEADS UP

The ginger syrup needs to cool before using it in drinks. It can be prepared up to 2 weeks ahead.

In a small saucepan, combine the ginger, agave nectar, and water. Bring to a boil. Lower the heat and simmer until the liquid reduces to a light syrup, about 15 minutes. Remove the pan from the heat and let the ginger syrup cool completely. Strain the syrup into a container and refrigerate, covered, for up to 2 weeks.

Put the ginger syrup, lime juice, and sparkling water in a pitcher. Stir to combine. Serve the limeade over ice. Alternatively, to make the limeade one glass at a time, fill a tall glass with ice and add approximately 3 tablespoons ginger syrup, 2 tablespoons lime juice, and top with sparkling water. Stir to combine.

VARIATIONS For an adult cooler, add a splash of vodka to each glass.

If you do not have agave nectar, make the syrup with 1 cup sugar instead. The sweetness is a bit different and consequently you may need to add a little more lime juice to taste.

Blueberry Drinking Vinegar

 MAKES 7 CUPS

After my first taste of drinking vinegar at a sushi restaurant in Tokyo, I instantly faced a new addiction. The drink, fruit-infused vinegar—a perfect balance of tart, sweet, and fruity—topped with club soda was utterly refreshing. I started noticing bottled fruit vinegars at Asian markets, but oddly enough many of them contained added gluten. To fuel my addiction I knew I had to learn to make it at home. Although it takes some time, the process is quite easy: macerate fruit—preferably organic—in vinegar, boil it with sugar, and strain. Once the infusion is chilled, enjoy it mixed with sparkling water.

10 cups fresh or frozen blueberries

3 cups distilled white vinegar

2 cups granulated sugar

Sparkling water or club soda, for serving

HEADS UP
The fruit in this recipe needs to macerate for 4 days.

Put the blueberries in a large container with a lid and mash them lightly with a potato masher or the back of a large spoon. Add the vinegar and stir. Cover the container and leave it on the counter for 4 days, stirring it once a day.

Pour the blueberry mixture into a pot and add the sugar. Bring to a boil. Lower the heat and simmer for 30 minutes. Taste the mixture; it should have a pleasant balance of sweet and tart. (Be careful. If you slurp it quickly while it's hot you will start coughing.) Stir in a bit more sugar if needed. Let the mixture cool and then strain it, pushing down on the fruit with the back of a spoon, into wide-mouth jars or another container with a lid. Refrigerate the drinking vinegar until chilled. It will keep for several months in the refrigerator.

For serving, pour about 1/4 cup of drinking vinegar over ice in a tall glass. Top with sparkling water or club soda. Stir to combine.

VARIATIONS I have tasted many varieties of drinking vinegar, but the only other versions I've made are cherry, raspberry, and peach—all delicious. Experiment with your favorite, altering the amount of sugar, as necessary, to match the sweetness of the fruit.

Plum Wine Sangria

 SERVES 10 TO 12

A friend recently brought over a bottle of umeshu, or plum wine, made from steeping ume (a Japanese fruit similar to plums) in alcohol and sugar. The resulting wine tastes slightly sweet and fruity, perfect as a light aperitif or even better mixed into a batch of festive sangria. I've had luck finding plum wine in the wine section of upscale groceries—it usually sits on the shelf right next to the sake—and it's certainly available at Asian markets as well. If you find a bottle that still has the ume or plum in it, go ahead and add that to your sangria.

1 cup diced pineapple

1 cup raspberries or blackberries

1 cup peeled and diced peaches

1 (750-ml) bottle umeshu or plum wine

1 (750-ml) bottle Prosecco or other sparkling wine

Sparkling water or club soda, for serving (optional)

HEADS UP
The sangria needs to chill for several hours before serving.

Put the fruit in a large pitcher or a punch bowl. Pour in the plum wine and Prosecco. Refrigerate for a few hours for the flavors to mingle and the sangria to chill. Pour the sangria into ice-filled glasses. Use a spoon to add some of the fruit to each glass. Top with a splash of sparkling water for a lighter refreshing drink.

VARIATION Try the sangria with other types of fruit: diced plums, green apple, or grapes would all taste great. Use about 3 cups diced fruit.

Plum Wine Sangria ↑

Blackberry Sake Mojito ↑

Sparkling Ginger Limeade ↑

Blackberry Sake Mojito

 SERVES 4

This riff on typical rum-based mojitos includes fragrant summer blackberries and a healthy splash of sake. I like mint flavor in a cocktail without the interference of the mint leaves, so I infuse the mint first in a simple syrup. This recipe makes a little more than 1/3 cup syrup. You only need 1/2 tablespoon for each mojito, so you can save the rest for another round of drinks or use it to sweeten iced tea. Find sake in the wine section of your grocery store or, for a larger selection, at Asian markets.

1/4 cup sugar

1/4 cup water

1/4 cup packed fresh mint leaves

3/4 cup blackberries

1/4 cup freshly squeezed lime juice

1 cup medium-dry sake

Sparkling water or club soda, to taste

HEADS UP

The mint syrup needs to chill and infuse for at least 15 minutes and up to several hours. You can prepare it up to 2 weeks ahead.

In a small saucepan, bring the sugar and water to a boil. Simmer until the sugar dissolves, about 1 minute. Put the mint in a 1-cup glass measure and pour the hot syrup over it. Transfer the measuring cup to the refrigerator to chill the syrup while it infuses, for at least 15 minutes and up to several hours. Or you can put it in the freezer for a quicker chill. The syrup will keep, covered, in the refrigerator for up to 2 weeks, but strain the mint after a few hours.

Divide the blackberries among 4 glasses. Pour 1 1/2 teaspoons mint syrup in each glass. Smash the berries and syrup together with a fork. Add ice to the glasses. Pour 1 tablespoon lime juice and 1/4 cup sake over the ice in each glass. Stir to combine. Top with sparkling water to taste.

Cucumber Saketini

 SERVES 1

Considering my fondness for drinking good sake, I hesitated to mar the experience by adding flavors. But I also enjoy cocktails, and a faint hint of cucumber complements the sake without overwhelming it. Despite the touch of agave nectar, this is not a sweet cocktail, but one for grown-up palates.

½ lime, cut into 4 wedges

1 (2-inch) segment peeled cucumber, plus 1 cucumber slice for garnish

1 teaspoon light agave nectar or simple syrup (see Heads Up)

¼ cup medium-dry sake

Put the lime wedges and then the cucumber in a cocktail shaker and smash them with a muddler or a fork. Add a handful of ice cubes, the agave nectar, and the sake. Cover and shake vigorously for 30 seconds. Strain the cocktail into a chilled martini glass. Garnish with a thin slice of cucumber.

HEADS UP

If you don't have agave nectar, make a simple syrup: Simmer equal parts sugar and water until the sugar dissolves. Refrigerate, covered, for up to 2 weeks.

Lychee Sorbet

 SERVES 6 TO 8

Have you ever tasted a lychee? They have the most intriguing sweet, floral taste, unlike any other fruit I've tried. Fresh ones are hard to find, but canned lychees work perfectly for the sorbet. Canned lychees generally come peeled and seeded, though the label rarely says so; do double-check before tossing them into the food processor. Tiny bits of fruit make the sorbet a bit chewy with a slightly more interesting texture than a completely smooth version. A single drop of red food coloring lends a lovely pink tint to the sorbet, but you can just as easily leave it natural.

1/2 cup sugar

1/4 cup water

2 (20-ounce) cans lychees, drained

1 drop red food coloring (optional)

HEADS UP

The sorbet base must chill completely, at least 4 hours or overnight. You need an ice cream maker or ice cube trays for this recipe.

In a small saucepan, combine the sugar and water. Bring to a boil over medium heat, stirring occasionally to dissolve the sugar. Boil for about 1 minute, until the syrup is clear. Remove the pan from the heat.

Puree the lychees in a food processor or a blender. You should have 2 cups lychee puree. Transfer the puree to a bowl and mix in the sugar syrup and the food coloring. Cover and refrigerate until completely chilled, at least 4 hours and up to overnight.

Freeze the sorbet in an ice cream maker according to the manufacturer's instructions. Cover and store in the freezer until ready to serve.

VARIATION If you don't have an ice cream maker, freeze the chilled sorbet base in ice cube trays. Once the cubes are frozen, pop them in a food processor or blender and puree. Return the sorbet to the freezer until ready to serve. This method won't yield quite as much sorbet (the ice cream maker incorporates air into the mix), but it's plenty for 4 servings.

Coconut Ice Cream

 MAKES ABOUT 1 QUART

If you're a fan of coconut ice cream, this is a must-try. It blows away any store-bought version I've tasted—and it's dairy free. Warning: The ice cream is incredibly rich! Sometimes I top it with sliced strawberries and sprinkle the toasted coconut on top instead of mixing it into the ice cream. You could use fresh pineapple as well for another tasty sundae. If you're on a sugar kick, reserve the egg whites (or even freeze them) for Thai Coffee Macarons (page 190).

2 (14-ounce) cans unsweetened coconut milk

6 large egg yolks

1²/₃ cups sugar

2 teaspoons vanilla extract

Pinch of salt

¹/₃ cup shredded coconut, toasted (optional) (see Heads Up)

HEADS UP
The ice cream base must chill completely, at least 4 hours and preferably overnight. You need an ice cream maker for this recipe.

To toast coconut: Spread shredded coconut on a baking sheet and bake at 350°F until golden brown, about 7 minutes. Keep an eye on it so it doesn't burn.

Heat the coconut milk in a saucepan over medium heat until steaming, about 4 minutes. Meanwhile, whisk the egg yolks with the sugar in a heatproof bowl. Slowly whisk the steaming coconut milk into the egg yolks (keep whisking so the eggs don't scramble), and then return the mixture to the pan. Cook over medium heat, stirring constantly, until the custard is thick enough to coat the back of a spoon (if you have a thermometer, it should read 180°F), 6 to 8 minutes (at this point you should be able to draw a line with your finger through the custard that doesn't drip or run).

Strain the custard into a bowl using a fine mesh strainer. Whisk in the vanilla and the salt. Cover and refrigerate until well chilled, at least 4 hours or up to overnight. More time equals more flavor. Freeze the ice cream in an ice cream maker according to the manufacturer's directions, adding the toasted coconut during the last 5 minutes of freezing. Cover and store in the freezer until ready to use.

VARIATION For a lighter version, use 1 can of regular coconut milk and 1 can of light coconut milk.

Mango *with Sweet Rice and Coconut Sauce*

 SERVES 8

Even before I was gluten free, mango with sweet rice topped my list of favorite desserts. Although it's good any way you serve it, I like the contrast of cold mangoes and coconut sauce over the warm rice. If you're serving it immediately you could put the sauce in the freezer for a quick chill. The recipe makes quite a bit; if you're only serving four, cook 1 cup of raw rice instead of 2. I would leave the sauce recipe the same (fold only ½ cup into the warm rice) and enjoy any leftovers over sliced fruit, such as pineapple, kiwi, papaya, or mango.

Sticky rice (page 101)

1 (14-ounce) can unsweetened coconut milk

¹/₂ cup sugar

Scant ¹/₂ teaspoon salt

1 teaspoon vanilla extract

2 ripe mangoes, diced, or 2 (10-ounce) packages diced frozen mango, defrosted but chilled

HEADS UP

The dish calls for sticky rice. It needs to soak for a minimum of 3 hours, preferably longer, before cooking.

While the rice is cooking, gently heat the coconut milk in a small saucepan just to a simmer, stirring occasionally. (*Note:* If you don't stir it you may end up with a coconut milk volcano. I know this firsthand.) Do not let the milk boil. Stir in the sugar, salt, and vanilla and cook until the sugar dissolves, about 1 minute longer. Set aside 1 cup of the sauce. Pour the remaining sauce into a bowl or a small pitcher and refrigerate (or quick chill in the freezer) until ready to use.

Transfer the rice to a large bowl. Pour the reserved coconut sauce over the rice and gently combine using a spatula. Cover the bowl with a towel and let the rice stand for at least 15 minutes and up to 3 hours to absorb the sauce. Spoon the rice into serving bowls and top with some of the mango. Stir the remaining (chilled) coconut sauce and pour some over each serving.

VARIATION Instead of mango, use another tropical fruit, such as pineapple, kiwi, or papaya. You will need 2 to 3 cups diced fruit.

Five-Spice Berry Crisp

 SERVES 6 TO 8

Admittedly, I have never seen a recipe for berry crisp on any Asian menu, but I was messing around during the bountiful Oregon berry season and came up with something tasty. Five-spice powder cooked into a batch of blackberries lends an exotic note to the fruit. I especially like the spice with the jammier blackberries and blueberries, but I included raspberries in the mix for added sweetness. Use whatever combination of berries you like as long it measures 6 cups. If you are averse to seeds definitely increase the amount of blueberries. Look for coconut oil alongside the other oils in natural food markets or upscale groceries. The oil comes in a jar or a small tub; it is solid at room temperature.

³/₄ **cup old-fashioned rolled oats** GF

¹/₃ **cup packed brown sugar**

¹/₄ **cup plus 2 tablespoons white rice flour**

4 tablespoons cornstarch, divided

¹/₄ **teaspoon salt**

¹/₂ **teaspoon Chinese five-spice powder, divided**

³/₄ **teaspoon ground cinnamon, divided**

6 tablespoons coconut oil

³/₄ **cup sliced almonds**

3 cups blackberries

2 cups blueberries

1 cup raspberries

¹/₃ **cup granulated sugar**

Preheat the oven to 400°F. Oil an 11 by 7-inch glass baking dish. In a medium bowl, combine the oats, brown sugar, rice flour, 2 tablespoons of the cornstarch, the salt, ¹/₄ teaspoon of the five-spice powder, and ¹/₂ teaspoon of the cinnamon. Add the coconut oil and rub the mixture together with your fingertips until coarse crumbs form. Stir in the almonds. Refrigerate until ready to use. (The topping can be refrigerated, covered, for 2 days or frozen for 1 month.)

Put the berries in the prepared baking dish. Sprinkle the granulated sugar and the remaining 2 tablespoons cornstarch, ¹/₄ teaspoon five-spice powder, and ¹/₄ teaspoon cinnamon evenly over the berries. Toss gently to combine. Sprinkle the oat mixture evenly over the berries. Bake until the topping is crisp and brown and the fruit is bubbling, 45 to 50 minutes. If the topping browns too quickly, lower the heat to 375°F. Cool slightly before serving.

VARIATIONS If dairy is part of your diet, you can use butter instead of the coconut oil.

If you have trouble finding five-spice powder, substitute 1¹/₄ teaspoons cinnamon instead (³/₄ teaspoon in the topping and ¹/₂ teaspoon with the berries). You will lose the exotic note, but it will still taste great.

Cook the crisp in individual gratin dishes or ramekins, set on a baking sheet. Start checking for doneness after about 35 minutes.

Thai Coffee Macarons

 **MAKES 16 SANDWICH COOKIES**

Let me tell you a little secret—I don't bake. But I really, really wanted to include a special meal-ending treat, so I enlisted Kyra Bussanich, owner of the delectable Crave Bake Shop in Portland, to help develop our cookie. She created a coffee ganache sandwiched between chocolate almond macarons. Not only is this one delicious cookie, but it's a gluten- and dairy-free one to boot.

Try to find a finely ground almond flour for your cookies. Trader Joe's makes a great one, as does Honeyville. Should you find yourself with extra ganache, heat it up and serve it as chocolate sauce over Coconut Ice Cream (page 186) or as a dip for strawberries; spoon some into your morning coffee for a decadent mocha; or just give in and eat it with a spoon.

1 cup dairy-free dark chocolate chips

1 cup unsweetened coconut milk

1 tablespoon instant espresso powder

$^1/_2$ cup almond flour (also called almond meal)

$^1/_4$ cup unsweetened cocoa powder

1 cup powdered sugar

3 large egg whites, at room temperature

$^1/_8$ teaspoon cream of tartar

$^1/_4$ cup granulated sugar

HEADS UP

The ganache needs to cool for 1 hour. You can prepare it up to 2 weeks ahead.

To make the ganache: Put the chocolate chips in a heatproof bowl. Heat the coconut milk and espresso powder in a small saucepan over medium heat until steaming, about 4 minutes. Pour the hot espresso milk over the chocolate chips and stir gently until the chocolate melts. Set aside to cool for at least an hour until the ganache is thick and spreadable. (The ganache can be made ahead. Refrigerate, covered, for up to 2 weeks.)

To make the macarons: Line 2 baking sheets with parchment paper or a silicone mat. Fit a pastry bag with a plain round piping tip, or substitute a gallon-size resealable bag.

Put the almond flour in the bowl of a food processor and process for 5 seconds. Add the cocoa powder and pulse to combine it with the almond flour. Add the powdered sugar and process for 10 to 15 seconds to eliminate any lumps.

Combine the egg whites and the cream of tartar in a clean mixing bowl. Using a freestanding or handheld electric mixer, beat the egg whites on medium speed until soft peaks form— there will be tiny bubbles and a white cloudlike appearance, not a foamy one. With the mixer on, pour the granulated sugar into the egg whites in a slow, steady stream. Continue beating the meringue to glossy medium peaks. It will be ready when you dip the whisk into the meringue and a floppy hook forms at the end of the whisk, which falls over when gently shaken.

Detach the bowl from the mixer and sprinkle in one-third of the dry ingredients. Using a spatula, gently fold the dry ingredients into the meringue until 90 percent incorporated. Sprinkle in half of the remaining dry ingredients and fold in until 90 percent incorporated. Add the remaining dry ingredients, folding until well incorporated. The batter should be an even color with no light or dark streaks.

Fill the pastry bag or resealable bag with the batter. (If using a plastic bag, seal the top and then cut off one of the bottom corners with scissors.) Pipe about 32 silver dollar–size dots onto the prepared baking sheets. The tops of the piped batter should look smooth; if they look a little lumpy, gently smooth the tops with a wet finger. Let the batter sit on the baking sheets for about 20 minutes to form a smooth, shiny skin. Preheat the oven to 350°F while the cookies rest.

Bake the macarons until you can gently tap on the top of each cookie without breaking the shell, 12 to 15 minutes. Remove the pan from the oven. If using parchment paper, let the cookies cool on the pan for 2 minutes before transferring them to a wire rack. If using a silicone mat, let the cookies cool completely on the pan.

Match up each cookie with a partner of roughly the same size and shape. Spread about 2 teaspoons of the coffee ganache on one side of each pair and gently press the cookies together to form a sandwich. The sandwich cookies can be prepared up to 2 days ahead, stored in an airtight container at room temperature. The filling in the assembled cookies will keep longer if the cookies are stored in the refrigerator, but the cookie will turn soggy faster. It's your call.

Mail Order Sources

Missing an ingredient? You can find almost anything these days via mail order. If you don't see the item you need listed below, a quick Internet search will likely uncover it.

Amazon
amazon.com
shichimi togarashi, split mung beans (*moong dal*), sesame tahini, agave nectar, coconut oil

A Taste of Thai
atasteofthai.com
coconut milk, curry paste, rice noodles, jasmine rice, peanut sauce, fish sauce, sweet chili sauce

Bob's Red Mill
bobsredmill.com
white rice flour, tapioca flour, sweet rice flour, cornstarch, millet flour, baking powder, xanthan gum, gluten-free oats, almond flour, potato starch

Eden Foods
edenfoods.com
bonito flakes, kombu, mirin, miso paste, noodles (cellophane/mung bean, rice, and 100 percent buckwheat soba) nori, pickled ginger, wheat-free tamari, dried shiitake mushrooms

The Ginger People
gingerpeople.com
pickled sushi ginger

Glutenfree.com
glutenfree.com
Premier Japan hoisin and teriyaki sauces, Kari-out individual gluten-free soy sauce packets, San-J wheat-free tamari, dairy-free chocolate chips, chicken broth, vanilla extract

Honest Foods
honestfoods.com
Wok Mei oyster, plum, and hoisin sauces

Huy Fong
huyfong.com
Sriracha sauce

KOA Mart
koamart.com
Korean crushed red pepper (fine and coarse), kimchi, sweet potato noodles (listed as Korean-style starch noodles), rice paper (spring roll wrappers), rice noodles, cellophane/mung bean noodles, sliced rice cakes (listed as *dduckgook*), tofu, sweet rice, Japanese rice

Koda Farms
kasakoda.com
Mochiko Blue Star sweet rice flour, rice flour, sushi rice, sweet rice

Lan Chi Foods
lanchifoods.com
black bean sauce with chili, chili paste with soybean, chili paste with garlic

Melissa's
melissas.com
dried wood ear, dried shiitake mushrooms, chiles, daikon radish, galangal, Japanese eggplant, kimchi, tofu

Pacific Foods
pacificfoods.com
chicken broth, mushroom broth

Penzeys Spices
penzeys.com
Chinese five-spice powder, whole star anise, and all of the more common spices

San-J
san-j.com
Wheat-free tamari, teriyaki sauce, peanut sauce, and single-serving wheat-free tamari packets

Temple of Thai
templeofthai.com
lemongrass, galangal, kaffir lime leaves, Thai basil, Erawan sweet rice, rice, and tapioca flours, split yellow mung beans (*moong dal*), rice paper wrappers (spring roll wrappers), rice noodles, cellophane/mung bean noodles, jasmine rice, sticky rice

Thai Kitchen
thaikitchen.com
peanut satay sauce, fish sauce, curry paste, rice noodles, coconut milk, sweet red chili sauce

The Wok Shop
wokshop.com
woks, steamers, Chinese wire mesh strainer, stir-frying tools, benriner slicers, ginger graters

Acknowledgments

It would have been virtually impossible for me to write *The Gluten-Free Asian Kitchen* without the tremendous support of my family, dear friends, and colleagues. Great thanks and appreciation to each and every one of you for your contributions, from research and recipe testing to the occasional offer of childcare. My heartfelt thanks to:

Patrick, the hardest working husband around. His commitment to our family enables me to pursue a career I love. He offers support in every way, including tasting, dish duty, proofreading, and patient (yet repeated) tech support. We've had an amazing journey.

William and Audrey, the greatest kids on the planet and quite possibly the most genuinely honest and harshest critics around. Any dish that passes their muster is an instant keeper. They demonstrated real patience while I cooked my way through Asia and now I will make them lots of pizza.

My parents, Sharon and Steve Byrne, for joining my sisters and me at the dinner table every *single* night while we were growing up. An amazing feat even then, it is now almost a lost art.

Marcia Faulhaber and Susan Rossi, my awesome sisters and dear friends. They keep me in line and sometimes they even make "yummy" noises when they eat my food, the most endearing quality a person could have.

My devoted tasting and testing team, many of whom sat at my kitchen counter week after week, sampling food, offering insightful critique, and then reevaluating the results until the job was done. Their commitment to the task was admirable, if not a little scary. These friends checked my work in their own kitchens, using their (gluten-loving) families as guinea pigs for the majority of the recipes in the book. Some even hosted dinner parties based on my recipes. (How fun is that?!) A thousand thank-yous to Catarina Hunter, Laura Ford, Natasha Pereira, Barbara Cohen, Shelby Quintos, Susan Terrell, Shawn Hunter, Ashley Campion, Sarah Remy, Ben Conte, Sara Conte, Marcia Faulhaber, Chris Faulhaber, John Laurent, Lefty Head, Sally Mays, Lynne Asgharzadeh, Meghan Pence, Nicole Grayson, Leslie Goss, Chrys Hutchings, Dave Boston, Kirsten Griffith, Leslie Mahler, Carla Van Hoomissen, Carey Wendle, Dan Wendle, Paula McCormick, and Lanelle Fechner.

Dr. Samantha Brody, Portland naturopath extraordinaire, without whose keen intuition I would still be walking around, numb, munching on gluten.

Torie Laurent, friend and owner of Indulge Catering in Portland, for her especially skillful way of cooking while balancing a four-month-old baby on one hip. Special thanks for developing the wildly delicious roasted pork meatballs.

Pastry chef and master of all things sweet, Kyra Bussanich, owner of Crave Bake Shop in Portland, Oregon. Kyra created several of the delectable desserts in this book and fielded many dough-related inquiries from an author lacking the baking gene.

My agent, Sharon Bowers, for making the process seamless.

Cookbook author Diane Morgan, who so generously and unselfishly shares her knowledge and expertise she could single-handedly inspire an entire generation of food writers! My book proposal would not have been the same without her stamp of approval.

Martha Holmberg, who, during her tenure as editor of the Oregonian's *FoodDay*, was gracious enough to green-light my column, one based entirely on gluten-free food. She is an insightful editor and a truly fun person.

Friend and fellow food writer Tami Parr for assuring me I could write and then graciously lending her editing skills—just in case.

Japanese food expert and cookbook author Elizabeth Andoh for thoroughly informative and thought-provoking conversations about Japanese ingredients.

Mrs. Yong Ja Chung and Yun Jae Chung for getting me hooked on Korean food many years ago, and more recently enduring my endless questioning about their recipes and techniques.

Dr. Kim Song for her tremendously educational hands-on kimchi tutorial. I may never buy kimchi again!

Abbie Hebein and Jessica Himelfarb, tireless research assistants, who gave me time to focus on the big stuff.

Lucy Eklund and April Eklund of Jade: Bistro, Teahouse, and Patisserie in Portland for sharing their love of Vietnamese cuisine and teaching me how to make *banh bot loc* and *banh cuon*.

Jimmy James Lang, my man on the ground in Bangkok, ever willing to try a traditional Thai dish in the name of research.

Sake expert Marcus Pakiser of P&S Wine Company, a division of Young's Columbia Oregon, for his astute introduction to sake.

Megan Cairns, Trish Mesch, Marco Rossi, Kerrie Ostrander, and Alan Stevenson (Diane's Natural Market in Saint Augustine, Florida) for their "field research" locating gluten-free products in stores across the country.

Andy Spencer and Pete Bronski for answering technical questions relating to gluten-free labeling and testing.

Designer Toni Tajima for giving the book pizzaz.

Photographer Leo Gong, food stylist Karen Shinto, and their teams for bringing the food to life.

Copy editor Molly Jackel and proof reader Karen Levy for catching my mistakes.

My amazing editor Jenny Wapner for guiding me through the steps and letting me keep my voice.

Aaron Wehner, publisher of Ten Speed Press, for willingly taking on a project that was not only gluten free, but Asian as well.

Bibliography

Alford, Jeffrey, and Naomi Duguid. *Hot Sour Salty Sweet: A Culinary Journey Through Southeast Asia.* New York: Artisan, 2000.

Alford, Jeffrey, and Naomi Duguid. *Seductions of Rice.* New York: Artisan, 1998.

Andoh, Elizabeth. *Washoku: Recipes from the Japanese Home Kitchen.* Berkeley: Ten Speed Press, 2005.

Bhumichitr, Vatcharin. *Vatch's Southeast Asian Cookbook.* New York: St. Martin's Press, 1997.

Dunlop, Fuchsia. *Land of Plenty: Authentic Sichuan Recipes Personally Gathered in the Chinese Province of Sichuan.* New York, London: W.W. Norton & Company, 2001.

Dunlop, Fuchsia. *Revolutionary Chinese Cookbook: Recipes from Hunan Province.* New York, London: W.W. Norton & Company, 2006.

Duong, Binh and Marcia Kiesel. *Simple Art of Vietnamese Cooking.* New York: Prentice Hall Press, 1991.

Hepinstall, Hi Soo Shin. *Growing Up in a Korean Kitchen: A Cookbook.* Berkeley, Toronto: Ten Speed Press, 2001.

Lee, Cecilia Hae-Jin. *Eating Korean: From Barbecue to Kimchi, Recipes from My Home.* Hoboken: John Wiley & Sons, Inc., 2005.

Marks, Copeland. *The Korean Kitchen: Classic Recipes from the Land of the Morning Calm.* San Francisco: Chronicle Books, 1993.

Nguyen, Andrea. *Asian Dumplings: Mastering Gyoza, Spring Rolls, Samosas, and More.* Berkeley: Ten Speed Press, 2009.

Nguyen, Andrea. *Into the Vietnamese Kitchen: Treasured Foodways, Modern Flavors.* Berkeley: Ten Speed Press, 2006.

Oseland, James. *Cradle of Flavor: Home Cooking from the Spice Islands of Indonesia, Malaysia, and Singapore.* New York, London: W.W. Norton & Company, 2006.

Shimbo, Hiroko. *The Japanese Kitchen: 250 Recipes in a Traditional Spirit.* Cambridge: Harvard Common Press, 2000.

Simonds, Nina. *Asian Noodles: Deliciously Simple Dishes to Twirl, Slurp, and Savor.* New York: Hearst Books, 1997.

Sodsook, Victor. *True Thai: The Modern Art of Thai Cooking.* New York: William Morrow and Company, Inc., 1995.

Thompson, David. *Thai Food.* Berkeley, Toronto: Ten Speed Press, 2002.

Trang, Corinne. *Authentic Vietnamese Cooking: Food from a Family Table.* New York: Simon & Schuster, 1999.

Trang, Corinne. *Noodles Every Day: Delicious Asian Recipes from Ramen to Rice Sticks.* San Francisco: Chronicle Books, 2009.

Tropp, Barbara. *The Modern Art of Chinese Cooking.* New York: Hearst Books, 1982.

Yagihashi, Takashi. *Takashi's Noodles.* Berkeley: Ten Speed Press, 2009.

Yin-Fei Lo, Eileen. *Mastering the Art of Chinese Cooking.* San Francisco: Chronicle Books, 2009.

Young, Grace. *The Wisdom of the Chinese Kitchen: Classic Family Recipes for Celebration and Healing.* New York: Simon & Schuster Editions, 1999.

Index

Published in the United States by Ten Speed Press, an imprint of the Crown Publishing Group,
a division of Random House, Inc., New York.
www.crownpublishing.com
www.tenspeed.com

Ten Speed Press and the Ten Speed Press colophon are registered trademarks of Random House, Inc.

Library of Congress Cataloging-in-Publication Data on file with the publisher.
Russell, Laura Byrne.
The gluten-free Asian kitchen: recipes for noodles, dumplings, sauces, and more / Laura Byrne Russell.
       p. cm.
Summary: "100 gluten-free recipes focused exclusively on the cuisines of China, Korea, Japan, Thailand, and
Vietnam"—Provided by publisher.
Includes bibliographical references and index.
1. Gluten-free diet—Recipes. 2. Cooking, Asian. I. Title.
RM237.86.R86 2011
641.5'638—dc22
                    2011004434

ISBN 978-1-58761-135-3

Cover and text design by Toni Tajima
Food styling by Karen Shinto
Prop styling by Carol Hacker

Printed in China
10 9 8 7 6 5 4 3 2 1
First Edition